SCIENCE EXPERIENCES
with Everyday Things

Howard R. Munson

Fearon Teacher Aids
a division of
David S. Lake Publishers
Belmont, California

ISBN 0-8224-6846-8

Printed in the United States of America

1. 9 8 7 6 5 4 3 2

CONTENTS

INTRODUCTION

What is science? How should science be taught? To put it simply, science is something people *do*. It is a human enterprise. Scientists study the universe and all that it contains. They attempt to observe, record, and explain the objects and phenomena that surround us.

Because the universe is so vast, scientists specialize and confine their studies to narrow areas. Fields of science or specialized sciences have been created. Biologists study living things; geologists study the earth; chemists study the composition, structure, and properties of substances; and physicists study the interactions of matter and energy. Despite these and further specializations, all scientists tend to work in similar ways. If children are to learn science, they must be able to understand, appreciate, and practice the methods that scientists use.

Children should learn that scientists gather data by observing, measuring, and recording, and that scientists evaluate data by organizing, comparing, and analyzing. Children should learn that scientists generate ideas, make statements of facts, make hypotheses, test hypotheses, and propose theories. Children should learn that scientists work with great care and precision, making sure that every experiment they conduct and every observation they make is repeatable. Children should learn that scientists accept the fact that their view of the world is only as good as current knowledge and technology permits, and that scientific knowledge is tentative and open to revision.

How then should students learn these things? Students can learn facts and develop ideas by reading and hearing about the world around us. However, it is generally agreed that students learn more and comprehend better when they are actively involved and can make first-hand observations. When students are actively involved they can also develop the skills that are vital in scientific work—skills such as observing, recording, predicting, comparing, inferring, and concluding. These skills are learned through repeated practice.

Science Experiences with Everyday Things is filled with activities that will give your students the direct experience and practice they need. There are three basic types of experiences in this book—experiments, demonstrations, and open-ended activities. The experiments are designed to give students experience in problem solving and drawing conclusions based on data they observe and record. A problem or question is posed at the beginning of each experiment. Demonstrations are generally used to show a fact or prove a point, though sometimes they may be done to show students how to assemble or use various pieces of equipment. The demonstrations should be performed by you— and you will know the outcomes in advance. The open-ended activities are experiments that can be set up as a science-interest center or a learning station.

All the activities in this book require only simple and easy-to-obtain materials. If by some chance you have to make a purchase, the required materials can be bought inexpensively in supermarkets, drugstores, or discount department stores. Since the emphasis in this book is on everyday materials, chapters are arranged by principal material rather than topic.

A note on the measurements used in this book: Measurements are given in metric units *except* when the materials are available only in standard units. Examples include 3″ × 5″ index cards, ¼″-diameter dowels, and 8″ soda straws. If precise quantities are not necessary, common measures, such as "about a cup of water," may be used.

1 EXPERIENCES WITH PLASTIC FILM CANISTERS

Plastic film canisters—the kind that 35-mm film comes in—are easily obtained. Many amateur photographers have them lying around in great numbers because they seem too useful to throw away. This chapter contains ideas for some very stimulating science lessons that use film canisters. Most of the lessons call for black or opaque canisters with tight-fitting lids.

SHAKE AND MATCH

Problem

Can you identify a material without seeing it?

Purpose

To show that some unseen materials can be identified through the senses of hearing and touch. To develop skills in observation and comparison.

What You Need

For each group of two to four students:
— 2 opaque film canisters
— tray or open box to hold supplies
— 3-5 small containers
— 3-5 kinds of dry materials (such as rice, tapioca, salt, lentils, macaroni, or dried peas)

For the class:
— paper and pencils
— tape or stick-on labels

Procedure

Set up this experiment before class. For each group, fill a film canister halfway with one of the materials. Use a small piece of tape to label the canister. Snap the cover in place. Fill the small containers with small amounts of the materials (each container should hold a different material; one should contain the same material that is in the film canister). Place each group's containers and an empty film canister in a box or on a tray.

Show the students a sealed canister. Tell them the canister contains one of the materials from the tray. Then tell them they have to find out which material is in the canister *without* opening it. (If the students need further direction, point out that they can use the empty film canister to "test" the sound and weight of each material on the tray.) When each group comes to a conclusion about what is in the canister, the students may open it and evaluate their work.

Depending on the materials used, this activity can range in difficulty from easy to hard. The activity can also be modified slightly and set up as a science-interest station. To do this, fill pairs of opaque film canisters halfway with materials such as rice, salt, sand, buttons, puffed rice, doughnut-shaped cereal, loose tea, paper clips, and tacks. Use small pieces of tape or stick-on labels to number the canisters. (Make sure canisters with the same contents are not numbered consecutively.) Keep a record of what each canister contains.

Place the canisters on a table in the classroom. Tell the students they can shake and examine the canisters but that they cannot open them. Suggest that students make a list of the canisters that seem to make matching sounds.

After several students make lists, have a "grand opening." Let students lift off the lids and check the accuracy of their lists. Replace the opened canisters with new canisters that contain different materials. This open-ended activity can continue as long as students are interested.

DESCRIBING THE UNSEEN

Problem

How accurately can we describe objects we cannot see?

Purpose

To show that several properties of unseen materials can be determined using the senses of hearing and touch. To develop skills in observation.

What You Need

For each pair of students:
— opaque film canister

For the class:
— a marble for each canister (All marbles should be the same color, but there should be two sizes—large and small.)
— a marble that is different in color from the rest (can be large or small)
— tape or stick-on labels

Procedure

Before class, put large marbles in half of the canisters and small marbles in the remaining canisters. (One of these should be the marble of a different color.) Use tape or stick-on labels to number the canisters. Record the number of the canister that contains the different-colored marble.

Write the following directions on the chalkboard: 1. Without opening your canister, examine its contents as carefully as you can. 2. Do not attempt to name the object inside your canister. 3. After you have finished your observations, draw *to scale* the object inside your canister. 4. Find another canister in the room which contains an object similar to yours. Record the number of the canister. 5. Find a canister which contains an object different from yours. Record the number of the canister. 6. One canister contains an object different from all others in the room. Find it and record its number.

Hand out the canisters to pairs of students. Emphasize that students should not open the canisters until you tell them to. Encourage the class to discuss their observations. After sufficient time, have each group show its drawing. Also have the groups identify the canisters (by number) that contain objects like theirs and objects different from theirs. Then ask the students if they can identify the canister that contains the object that is different from all the rest. Write a list of their predictions on the chalkboard. Then tell them the number of the canister that contains the different-colored marble. Give the students time to examine the canister to see if they can determine how the contents are different.

Before students open their canisters, remind the class that they used the senses of hearing and touch to describe an unseen object. Explain that scientists frequently have similar tasks.

Now have students open the canisters and compare the contents with the drawings. Ask them why identifying the one different object was impossible. (The differing property—color—cannot be determined using the senses of hearing or touch.) Point out to the students that their results were limited because they lacked full knowledge of all the variables. They also lacked precise instruments to help them discover the variables. Explain that scientists often have to work in these conditions. They are limited not only by the capabilities and precision of their instruments, but by not knowing the "whole picture." As more knowledge and better instruments become available, our ideas about the world around us change.

FREEZING DIFFERENT LIQUIDS

Problem

Do all the liquids react in a similar way when frozen?

Purpose

To compare the effects of low temperature on different household liquids. To develop skills in observation and comparison.

What You Need

For each student:
− paper and pencil

For the class:
− 6–8 plastic film canisters with tight-fitting snap-on lids (Transparent canisters work best.)
− 6–8 different household liquids (such as water, milk, catsup, honey, rubbing alcohol, ammonia, liquid detergent, or cooking oil)
− freezer tray or foil-lined shoe-box lid
− portable cooler (if no freezer is available)
− 1–2 lb dry ice (if no freezer is available)

— piece of cardboard (if no freezer is available)
— tongs (if no freezer is available)
— tape or stick-on labels (optional)

Procedure

Discuss what happens when water is frozen. Point out that water expands when frozen. Ask students if they think other liquids will react the same way when frozen.

Fill each canister with a different liquid. If you use opaque canisters, label each one. Carefully snap on the covers and wipe off any excess liquid. Stand the canisters in the freezer tray or shoe-box lid. If a freezer is readily available, place the canisters in the freezer and leave them for twenty-four hours. Otherwise, use the tongs to place dry ice in the bottom of the cooler. Cover the ice with a piece of cardboard. Place the tray on the cardboard and put the lid on the cooler. *(Caution! Do not allow students to touch the dry ice.)* Leave the canisters for two or three hours.

After you have placed the canisters in the freezer, have students predict what will happen to each liquid. They should write down their predictions.

After freezing the canisters, remove the tray and have the students inspect the canisters without handling them. (If you used dry ice, remove the canisters with the tongs and let them sit at room temperature for fifteen minutes before handling them.) Ask questions such as "Did all the covers stay on?" "Which liquids were in the canisters with no lids?" "Why did the covers come off some of the canisters but not others?" Have students open the canisters and examine the contents. Ask them if the liquids reacted the way they predicted.

Point out that all liquids do not react the same way when frozen. For example, cooking oil will expand but will not solidify. Honey will usually crystallize without becoming completely solid. Milk or juice will freeze like water.

SOLAR HEAT AND BODY HEAT

Problem

Can we collect solar heat and body heat?

Purpose

To show that solar heat and body heat can be trapped and felt.

What You Need

For each student:
— black plastic film canister

Procedure

Do this experiment on a calm, sunny day when the temperature is between 8° C and 18° C. Have students stand in the sunlight holding up both their index fingers. Have each child place an inverted film canister over the index finger of one hand. After half a minute, ask students to compare how the covered and uncovered fingers feel. Most students will say the covered finger feels warmer.

Explain that two principles are involved in this simple experiment. First, the film canister traps body heat given off by the finger by preventing cool air from carrying the heat away. Second, the black color absorbs heat from the sun, which in turn heats the air inside the canister. The total result makes one finger warmer than the other. You might point out that the same results occur when people wear dark-colored clothes in the winter. Warm air is kept close to the body, and the dark colors absorb additional heat from the sun.

Also point out that one finger was left uncovered so it could be compared to the covered finger. Scientists would call the uncovered finger a *control* and the covered finger a *variable*. Most science experiments have controls and variables so changes can be easily seen and measured.

2 EXPERIENCES WITH PAPER AND PLASTIC BAGS

Paper and plastic bags, common items in every household, are especially useful when teaching science. Paper grocery bags are appropriate for experiments and demonstrations that require a bag that can remain in an open, upright position. Plastic bags are wonderful, easy-to-obtain, airtight and watertight containers.

The science activities in this section use either plastic or paper bags. Used or recycled bags will work in all cases as long as they do not have holes or tears.

MEASURING AIR EXPANSION

Problem

What happens to air as the temperature changes?

Purpose

To show that air expands when heated, and contracts when cooled.

What You Need

For each group of four students:
- plastic sandwich bag (Do not use press-seal type.)
- clear beverage bottle (at least 750 ml capacity)
- string (15 cm)
- 2 dish towels
- book
- metric ruler
- bowl of hot water (40°–45° C)

Procedure

Discuss the effects of heat on different materials. Ask students for examples of objects that are made in such a way that the materials have room to change size as the temperature changes. For example, sidewalks usually have tar-filled cracks between the pieces of concrete so the concrete has room to expand when it is hot. Also ask students if they can give you proof that the materials change size (for example, proof that the concrete slabs actually increase and decrease in size as the temperature changes). Point out that to get proof, the students would have to experiment.

Ask the students if they think air expands when it is heated. Tell them that they will do an experiment to see if they can prove that air expands.

Hand out the materials to each group. Have students tie the plastic sandwich bag tightly over the neck of the bottle. Have them lay the bottle on its side and place the plastic bag under the front cover of a book. (See Figure 1.) Have students measure and record the distance from the top front edge of the book cover to the table.

Figure 1

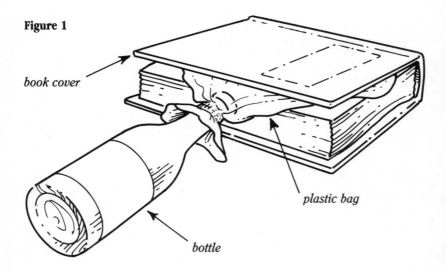

book cover

plastic bag

bottle

Have the students soak the towels in the hot water. They should wring out one towel and quickly wrap it around the bottle. As soon as the towel starts to cool, the students should replace it with the other heated towel. After five minutes, while a hot towel is still wrapped around the bottle, have the students measure and record the distance from the book cover to the table again. Students should let the bottle cool for five minutes and then remeasure the distance.

Once all the students have finished the experiment, ask them to describe their results. A typical response might be "Before heating the bottle, the book cover was 3.5 cm above the desk top. After heating the bottle for five minutes, the book cover was 5.4 cm above the desk top. After allowing the bottle to cool for five minutes, the book cover was 3.6 cm above the desk top." Ask students to explain why the change occurred and discuss their answers. Point out that the air in the bottle was heated when the hot towels were wrapped around the bottle. When air is heated, it expands. Since the bottle cannot expand enough to hold the heated air, the air from the bottle was pushed into the plastic bag. The plastic bag expanded and lifted up the edge of the book cover.

HEATING AIR

Purpose

To show that air expands when heated. To show that black surfaces absorb heat more effectively than light-colored or reflective surfaces.

What You Need

For the demonstration:
— black plastic trash bag
— white or silver-gray plastic trash bag (the same size as the black bag)
— masking tape or string
— twist-tie fasteners

Procedure

Partially inflate the black trash bag and tightly seal it with a twist-tie. Do the same with the white or silver-gray bag. The two bags should be about the same size. Place a strip of masking tape or tie a piece of string around the middle of each bag. Place the bags in bright sunlight, away from cooling air currents.

As the air in the bags is heated by the sun, the bags will expand. The black bag will expand more than the white or silver-gray bag. (See Figure 2.) Explain that black surfaces absorb heat. The air inside the bag is heated by contact with the bag surface. As the air is heated, it expands. White or silver-gray bags reflect some of the heat, so the air inside these bags will not be heated as much as the air in the black bag. The string or tape around each bag makes it easier to see how much the bag has changed due to heat.

This activity can also be done as a student investigation. Have students work in groups of two or three, with each group doing the activity. You might want students to try other colors of bags such as tan, green, and brown.

Figure 2

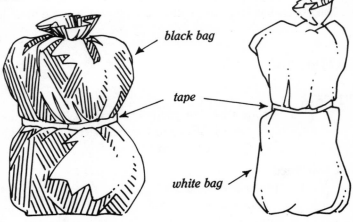

black bag

tape

white bag

WARM AIR RISES

Purpose

To show that warm air rises.

What You Need

For the demonstration:
- 2 paper bags of equal size (Large grocery bags work well.)
- 3 pieces of string (each 40 cm long)
- 2 small buttons
- meterstick or similar wood stick
- lamp with exposed 60-watt bulb

Procedure

Ask the students if they have ever seen balloon races or movies of balloon races. Point out that hot-air balloons have a burner at the base of the air bag. Ask students if they know why the burner is needed. Tell them that you are going to do a demonstration to show why balloons need the burners.

Open the two paper bags. Make a small hole in the center of the bottom of each bag. Push a piece of string through each hole and tie a button onto the end of the string that is inside the bag. Tie one paper bag to each end of the meterstick so both bags are upside down. (See Figure 3.) Tie another piece of string to the center of the stick and suspend the stick from an overhead support such as a light fixture. Balance the stick and bags so they hang evenly.

Figure 3

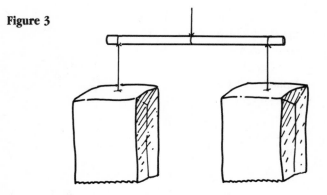

Turn on the lamp and hold it so the bulb is about halfway into one of the bags. Hold the lamp in place for several minutes. The bag over the bulb should rise and its movement should be visible.

Ask students if they can explain why the bag rose. Discuss their answers, and then tell them the light bulb heats the air in the inverted sack. The heated air expands, pushing some air molecules out of the bag. The air in the bag becomes less dense, and therefore lighter, than the air in the unheated bag. This causes the bag to rise.

Ask the class to use the results of this demonstration to tell you why hot-air balloons need burners. (A hot-air balloon needs a burner to heat the air inside the balloon. When the air is heated, the balloon rises. If the air inside the balloon cools too much, the balloon starts to descend, so the balloonist frequently does "short burns" to keep the balloon aloft. When the balloonist wants to land, he or she opens a flap or valve that lets hot air out of the balloon.)

A HEAVY GAS

Purpose

To show that carbon dioxide (CO_2) is heavier than air.

What You Need

For the demonstration:
— 2 paper bags of equal size (Large grocery bags will work well.)
— 3 pieces of string (each 40 cm long)
— meterstick or similar wood stick
— jar or pitcher (4 liter capacity)
— jar or pitcher (500 ml capacity)
— baking soda (300 g)
— vinegar (200 ml)
— water (200 ml)
— Plasticine
— tape

Procedure

Open the two paper bags and tape a piece of string to the back of each one. Tie one paper bag to each end of the meterstick. Then tie another piece of string to the center of the stick and suspend the stick from an overhead support such as a doorway. (See Figure 4.) Balance this apparatus by attaching small bits of Plasticine to one bag.

Put the baking soda in the 4 liter jar or pitcher. Mix the vinegar and water in the other container. Pour the liquids into the jar with the baking soda. There will be a great deal of fizzing and bubbling as the chemical reaction between baking soda and the vinegar begins. When the action slows, stir the mixture. The bubbles contain CO_2 gas. When the fizzing stops, no more gas is being generated.

CO_2 is heavier than air and it will displace the air in the large jar. While you cannot see the gas, the jar is nearly full of CO_2. It can be poured out of the jar as if it were liquid.

Carefully pour the gas into one of the bags—just pretend you are pouring a liquid. Be very careful not to pour out any of the actual liquid that is in the jar.

The CO_2 will displace some of the air in the bag. The bag will become heavier than the bag filled with air and the balance will be upset.

Figure 4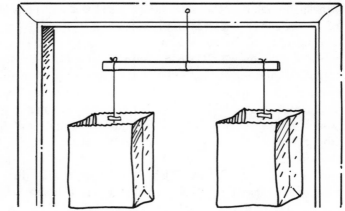

A SURPRISING EVENT

Purpose

To develop skills in making and testing hypotheses.

What You Need

For the demonstration:
- small plastic bag
- 3-4 round toothpicks
- well-sharpened round pencil
- well-sharpened hexagonal pencil
- pitcher of water

Procedure

Show students a plastic bag and ask them what they have used this type of bag for. Then ask the students to describe the properties of plastic bags. (For example, thin, can be sealed, transparent, and watertight.)

Select a student to help you with the demonstration. Have the helper hold the bag by its upper corners. Pour about 180 ml of water into the bag. Then slowly and steadily (don't jab), twist the round pencil through one side of the bag below the water line. *Leave the pencil in place.* The bag will not leak.

Using the same steady twisting motion, push several toothpicks into the bag (don't push them more than halfway in) and leave them in place. Do the same with the hexagonal pencil. Finally, push one of the pencils through the other side of the bag so the sharp end is on one side of the bag and the eraser is on the other.

Students will be amazed that the bag does not leak. They will probably ask you why. Do not answer or attempt to answer. Instead, initiate a question game. Tell students you want them to help you develop a list of questions that begin with the words "Will it work if . . ." and end with their ideas. Sample questions might be, "Will it work if you use a pencil with a dull point?" or "Will it work if the liquid in the bag is milk?" Have the students make a list of at least ten questions.

Once the students have finished their lists, explain that scientists have to experiment to find answers. Tell the students that they have to test as many of the ideas on their lists as they can. (This can be a home assignment or a classroom assignment.) Ask the students to report their results within two days.

Results of experimentation will show the following: 1. Plastic bags of any size or thickness will work. 2. Many kinds of liquids will work. 3. Smooth penetrating objects work better than rough ones. 4. Knife blades will cause a leak.

Through discussion, help students formulate a hypothesis that explains why the bag does not leak in certain circumstances. (It appears that the objects stretch the plastic just enough that the bag seals around them. Anything that causes a rough tear will cause a leak.)

3 EXPERIENCES WITH PAPER CLIPS

Ah, the lowly paper clip! It is the epitome of simplicity, yet it is a wonderfully versatile object. The activities described here require metal paper clips. For most of the activities, the paper clips should be 30-40 mm long and 7-8 mm wide.

BENDING AND BREAKING

Problem

Is the strength of metal in paper clips uniform?

Purpose

To develop skills in manipulating materials, recording data, organizing data, and drawing conclusions.

What You Need

For each group of four students:
- 5 paper clips of the same size and thickness
- 5 paper clips of different sizes and thicknesses
- 2 pairs of pliers

For the demonstration:
- pair of pliers
- paper clip, bobby pin, or section of coat hanger
- paper clip

Procedure

Begin by showing students that a piece of wire can be broken if it is repeatedly bent back and forth at the same point. After the bending demonstration, ask the students if they think the number of bends required to break objects like paper clips is uniform. If they say yes, ask them why they suspect there might be some uniformity. (They may say that paper clips from the same box seem to be made of the same material and are of similar thickness.)

Divide students into groups of four and hand out the materials. (If there is a problem giving each group two pairs of pliers, students can manipulate the wire with their fingers. However, this will produce less accurate results.)

Bend one end of a paper clip so it resembles Figure 5. Grip the paper clip with two pliers about 1 cm apart (points X and Y in figure 5). Bend the wire at point Y to a right angle and then back again. Do this until the wire breaks, counting the number of times you bend the wire.

Figure 5

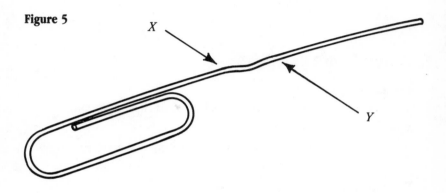

Record the number. Now ask students to follow the same procedure with their paper clips. When each student has broken a paper clip, develop a histogram on the chalkboard. Start the histogram by asking students to tell you the least number of bends and the greatest number of bends. For example, suppose the numbers are 3 and 8. Number vertically from 8 to 3 on the chalkboard. Next, have each student tell you the number of bends it took to break his or her paper clip. Record the number with an "x" by the appropriate numeral. (See Figure 6.) After the results are recorded, ask students what the histogram tells them about the uniformity of strength in paper-clip wire. Also ask them to predict the number of bends required to break the next paper clip from the same box. Show the class a much larger or smaller paper clip and ask them if they can predict the number of bends necessary to break it. Students should reason that they cannot make a prediction for a different type of paper clip. Have them break and bend other kinds of paper clips and compare their results.

Figure 6

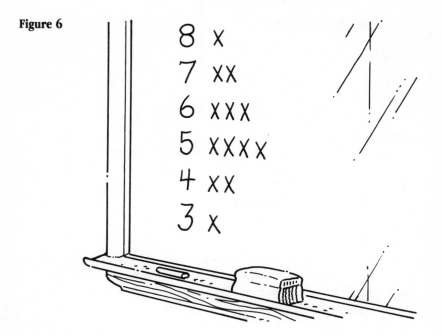

8 X
7 XX
6 XXX
5 XXXX
4 XX
3 X

After students have finished their manipulations, you might ask questions such as: "What are some materials that must withstand many, perhaps thousands, of bends daily?" "Why is lamp cord made of finely woven or wound wires rather than a solid copper wire the thickness of a paper clip?" "Does the speed at which you bend the wire influence the number of bends required the break the wire?" "Does the speed at which you bend the wire influence the temperature of the wire at the point where you bend it?" (Students can check this last question by bending the wire slowly several times and then quickly touching the wire at the point where it was bent, and then varying the procedure by bending the wire rapidly the same number of times. They should find that when the wire is quickly bent, the point will be warm or even hot to the touch. This shows that mechanical energy is being transformed into heat energy.)

This experiment shows that some materials can be weakened and eventually broken by repeated bending. It also shows that materials of similar size and composition are likely to have a relatively uniform resistance to breaking.

FULLER THAN FULL?

Problem

Is it possible to fill a cup beyond its rim?

Purpose

To show the surface tension of water.

What You Need

For each group of two or three students:
- 20-30 paper clips
- plastic cup
- pitcher of water
- aluminum pie tin

Procedure

Briefly discuss experiences students might have had with "heaping" measures. (They may recall seeing or hearing of recipes that call for a heaping teaspoon of salt or sugar.) Ask students if they think it's possible to have a "heaping" glass of water.

Have students place a cup in the pie pan. Then have them pour water into the cup until it is full to the rim. Then tell students to put one paper clip at a time into the cup—they should be careful not to drop the clips from high above the water. Have students look across the top of the cup after three or four paper clips have been added. They will see that the level of water has risen above the top of the cup and has formed a rounded or "heaping" surface.

After this phenomenon has been observed, students should continue to add paper clips to the water until the water spills. Have them count the number of clips that are in the cup.

Ask students if they can explain why the water did not spill as soon as the water reached the rim. Point out that water molecules are attracted to each other, and that the attraction between the surface water molecules draws them very close together. This forms a skinlike surface that keeps the water together. The "skin" also helps adhere the water to the rim of the glass. This makes it possible to build up water above the top of the cup. The "skin" will break when the weight of the water gets too heavy.

You might extend this activity by having students test other liquids. Challenge them to discover which liquid "heaps" the highest.

FLOAT A PAPER CLIP?

Problem

Is it possible to float a paper clip on water?

Purpose

To show the surface tension of water.

What You Need

For each group of two students:
- two standard-size paper clips
- clear plastic cup
- toothpick
- small amount of liquid detergent
- paper towels
- needle (optional)

Procedure

Have students fill their cups three-quarters full of water. Tell them to bend one paper clip open so it forms a right angle. Then have them lay the second paper clip across the "lap" of the first clip. (See Figure 7.) Students should make sure the water is very still, and then they should slowly and carefully lower the paper clips onto the water. The paper clip that lies across the bent paper clip should float.

Figure 7

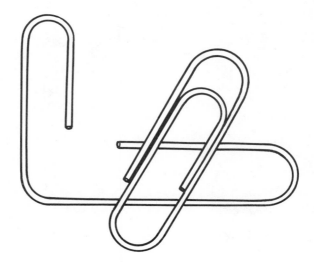

If the students' attempts are not successful, they should try again. (Wet paper clips should be dried on a paper towel before another attempt is made.) Have students try a needle if the paper clip does not float. Once some students succeed in floating the paper clip, they will probably want to help others. They should be encouraged to do so.

Tell students to look carefully at the surface of the water where the paper clip or needle rests. They will see that the floating object makes a slight indentation in the water's surface. Explain that water molecules cling together to form a surface that is strong enough to support a paper clip. This effect is called *surface tension*. All liquids show surface tension, though its strength varies from one liquid to another.

When all the students have a paper clip or needle floating on the water, tell them to touch one end of a toothpick in the liquid detergent and then to touch that end to the surface of the water. The paper clip will immediately sink. Say that this occurs because the detergent weakens the surface tension of the water so the water is no longer able to hold up the paper clip or needle.

4 EXPERIENCES WITH SODA STRAWS

What school-age child has not found an amusing or entertaining way to use soda straws? They have been used to launch straw-wrapper "rockets" and to blow bubbles in milk. They have also been used to blow soap bubbles, to build simple weather instruments, and to demonstrate air pressure.

In demonstrations and experiments, soda straws can be used to develop science skills and to teach important concepts and generalizations. The experiences in this chapter will give children opportunities to improve skills in observing, experimenting, predicting, recording data, generalizing, and drawing conclusions.

MOVING AIR

Problem

What causes the air in a room to move?

Purpose

To show that many activities cause air disturbances. To develop skills in observation, recording data, and drawing conclusions.

What You Need

For each student:
- soda straw (preferably plastic)
- tissue paper
- transparent tape
- scissors
- ruler

Procedure

If necessary, start the experiment by establishing that air is all around us. This concept is basic to the activity.

Ask the students whether the air in the room is still or moving. Then ask how they could find out whether the air is still or moving. Discuss their suggestions, and then show the class a previously prepared air-movement indicator. Point out that the tissue-paper strips move when the air moves. Ask students how this instrument could be used to observe air movements. Lead students into suggesting various things they could learn if each student placed an indicator on his or her desk and/or somewhere else in the classroom.

Hand out the materials and tell students how to make an indicator. Have them cut three or four pieces of tissue paper into 1 × 6 cm strips. Students should tape these pieces about ½ cm apart on one end of the straw. (See Figure 8.)

Figure 8

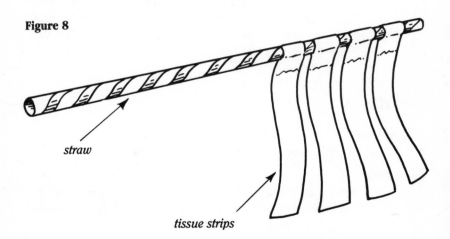

straw

tissue strips

Have some students attach their indicators to their desktops. The indicators should stick out from the side of the desk and extend into the walking space between desks. (See Figure 9.) Have the remaining students select other places for their indicators. For example, some indicators may be placed near the floor, some may be fastened to objects that are at the student's height, and some may be fastened near the ceiling. Tell students that they should observe their indicators from time to time and make a record of what happened in the room when the tissue strips moved. Eventually, their records might include reports such as "Person walked by," "Door opened," and "Book closed." Some constant movement may be caused by a heating unit or an open window. You might want to instruct students to ignore minor movement, or, if there is much constant movement, have the students move their indicators to a different place.

Figure 9

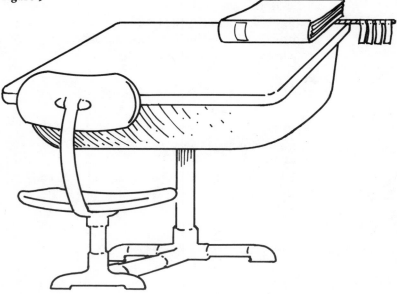

After a day or two of record keeping, the reports should be summarized and recorded on the chalkboard. Using this list, help students conclude that air movement is caused by many different activities in the room and that air is constantly in motion. Ask students if there is any value in having room air stirred by activity.

Once students reach the conclusion that air in the room is in motion, you might ask if this condition is true outside. Discuss some events that cause air to move out-of-doors. (Caution! Do not allow students to conclude that winds are caused by air movement. You might need to explain that winds occur because of temperature and pressure changes in the atmosphere.)

CHANGING THE FREQUENCY OF PENDULUM SWINGS

Problem

Is the number of times a pendulum swings in fifteen seconds determined by the pendulum's weight or by its length?

Purpose

To show that the frequency with which a pendulum swings is determined by its length. To develop skills in experimentation, organizing data, and drawing conclusions.

What You Need

For each group of four or five students:
— 10 plastic straws
— 10 straight pins or needles (at least 3 cm long)
— 16 uniform weights (such as pennies, nails, or washers)
— 2 pieces corrugated cardboard (each 30 × 30 cm)
— wood block (2 × 2 × 30 cm)
— tacks
— clear plastic tape

Procedure

Help each group make a pendulum stand. They should tack the two pieces of corrugated cardboard to the wood block. Then they should cut a 1-cm–deep notch, 2 cm from the end of each piece of cardboard. (See Figure 10.)

Next, have each group prepare ten pendulum arms. Have students cut two straws to each of the following lengths: 20 cm, 18 cm, 16 cm, 14 cm, and 12 cm. Students should tape a single weight onto the end of one straw of each length and tape three weights onto the ends of the remaining straws. Have students push a straight pin or needle through the free end of each straw, about 1 cm from the edge. (See Figure 11.) Have students create a free-moving pendulum by placing the pin ends of a 20-cm pendulum arm in the notches of the support.

Tell students to lift the arm to a 45° angle and let it drop. Ask them to observe the motion of the pendulum and describe what they see. Students will probably say that the distance the arm swings becomes shorter with each swing. Ask them if the speed of the swing seems to change (The speed of the swing does not change even though the weight moves less distance with each swing.)

Now ask students if they can think of a way to change the number of times the pendulum swings in fifteen seconds—that is, the frequency with which the pendulum swings. You might help them by asking whether changing the weight of the pendulum will change the frequency, and whether changing the length of the pendulum will change the frequency.

Figure 10

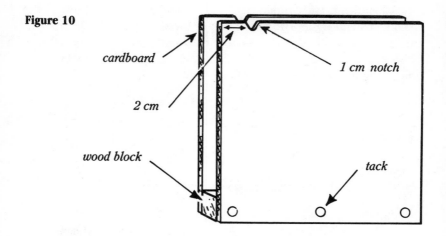

cardboard

2 cm

1 cm notch

wood block

tack

Figure 11

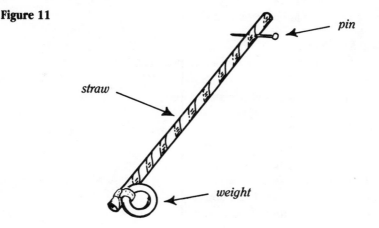

pin

straw

weight

Have the students test the 'pendulum arms they have prepared. Remind them to lift the arm to the same height each time. Tell students to count the number of swings (starting point to starting point) completed in fifteen seconds and to record the results for each pendulum arm.

After students have finished testing the pendulum arms, make a number line on a bulletin board or chalkboard. Number from 5 to 30, leaving about 3 cm between each numeral. Tape or pin each pendulum arm to the number line, placing it below the number of swings it completed in fifteen seconds.

Ask students what conclusions they can draw from the results. They should conclude that two pendulums of the same length have the same frequency regardless of the number of weights attached. They should also conclude that shorter pendulums have a greater frequency (more swings in fifteen seconds) than longer pendulums.

LAYERS OF LIQUIDS

Problem

How can you float water on top of water?

Purpose

To show that less dense liquids float on top of denser liquids. To develop skills in experimentation and manipulation of materials.

What You Need

For each group of four students:
— 4 clear plastic straws
— 4 paper or plastic cups
— table salt
— food coloring (four colors)
— measuring spoons
— pitcher of water

For the demonstration:
— clear plastic straw
— cup of colored water

Procedure

Discuss flotation with students. Ask them why wood, Styrofoam, leaves, and pieces of paper will float on water. Students will probably respond with answers that include the idea of weight. (For example, they may say that wood floats on water because it is lighter than water.) Explain that wood will float, as will other materials, if the wood's weight per unit of volume is less than that of water.

Ask students if they have ever seen one liquid float on another, such as oil floating on top of water or cream floating on top of milk. You might want to pour some cooking oil on water so students can observe this phenomenon. Tell the class that they will try to float water on water.

Before starting the experiment, demonstrate how to use a straw as a pipette. Put a straw into a cup of colored water, place one finger tightly over the open end of the straw, and lift it out of the cup. The liquid will stay in the straw until you lift your finger. Explain that this technique will be used to make layers of water.

Hand out the materials and instruct students to fill the four cups halfway with water. Then have them put ¼ teaspoon of salt in the first cup, ½ teaspoon of salt in the second cup, and ¾ teaspoon of salt in the third cup. Tell students to put about three drops of food coloring in each cup. (They should use a different color for each cup.) Have them stir the solutions well and make a record of what each cup contains (the amount of salt and the color).

Have students put a straw into the cup containing only water. They should lower the straw so approximately 1 cm is in the water. Then they should place a finger tightly over the top of the straw and lift it out of the cup. Tell them to keep a finger over the top of the straw while they lower the straw into a cup containing salt and food coloring. Now ask them to release the finger from the top, just for a moment, and then replace the finger over the top of the straw. Have students lift the straw and hold it to a light. They should see layers of liquid in the straw—the clear water should be on top of the colored water.

Once students have successfully layered the two liquids, they should experiment with the other salt solutions. You might guide them by asking questions such as: "Can you make a red solution float on top of clear water?" "Can you make three layers?" "Which solution floats on top of all the others?"

Point out that adding salt to the water increases the water's density. The more salt that is dissolved in water, the more dense the solution becomes. Less dense solutions will float on top of more dense solutions. (Note: In this experiment it is assumed that the food coloring does not change the density of the solutions. Actually, it does have an effect, though it is too slight to influence the results.)

SPEAR A SPUD

Purpose

To show that hollow tubes have great strength.

What You Need

For the demonstration:
- paper or plastic straws (Paper makes a better demonstration than plastic.)
- fresh, raw potato
- fresh, unwaxed apple

Procedure

Show students the straw. Ask them if they think it is possible to push the straw through a raw potato. You might let some students try.

Now, hold the potato so that if the straw slips or goes directly through the potato you will not hurt your hand. Grasp the straw and place your thumb over the top of the straw. Use a straight down motion (not an arc) to jab the straw into the potato. (You may have to practice this maneuver before showing it to the class.) The straw should go deep into the potato. Repeat the demonstration using an apple.

If you have problems getting the straw through the potato or apple, try holding the straw upright so one end rests on a table or desk and striking the potato against the end of the straw. Again, a straight down motion is necessary since an arcing motion will cause the straw to bend or buckle.

Explain that it is possible to penetrate the potato and apple with a straw because hollow tubes have a great deal of strength. You can demonstrate this by flattening the straw and trying to penetrate the potato. The straw will bend or buckle immediately.

5 EXPERIENCES WITH SPOOLS AND REELS

Spools and reels can be used as wheels. Perhaps that is one reason they are found so often in children's toy collections. A number of interesting, challenging, and productive activities can be developed through the use of thread spools, film spools, and old tape-recorder reels. The experiences here are just a few of the many possible creative and exciting spool and reel activities.

CHANGING THE PATH OF A ROLLING SPOOL

Problem

Is a rolling spool influenced by the surface it rolls on?

Purpose

To show that the path of a rolling spool can be influenced by the surface it rolls on. To develop skills in observation and prediction.

What You Need

For each group of four students:
— empty film spool
— smooth piece of heavy cardboard (at least 10 × 40 cm)
— 4 or 5 books
— fine sandpaper (No. 0 works well.)
— coarse sandpaper (No. 2 or No. 3 works well.)

Procedure

Begin by showing students how to set up the experiment. Stack the books on the floor or on a long table. Place one end of the cardboard on the books so the cardboard forms an inclined plane or ramp. Draw a mark near the top of the ramp to show the starting point of the spool. Then place the spool on the mark. Allow it to roll down the ramp and onto the table or floor until it stops by itself. The spool should roll straight down the ramp. If it doesn't, try again.

Once you have shown students the motion of the spool, ask them if they can think of anything that might cause the spool to change direction while it's rolling on the table. Students might suggest putting a pencil or some other objects in front of the spool. Try some of their suggestions.

Have each group set up a ramp. Ask the class to predict what would happen if a spool rolled onto an area where one rim was on a smooth surface and the other was on a rough surface. Write their predictions on the chalkboard. Then have each group put a piece of fine sandpaper about 10 cm from the end of the ramp so one rim of the rolling spool will be on the sandpaper and the other rim will be on the table or floor. (See Figure 12.) Have the students roll their spools several times so they can observe the path of a spool as it rolls across the sandpaper. (Students may need to practice rolling the spool to get the spool to roll straight down the ramp.) Once students have had time to observe the path of the

Figure 12

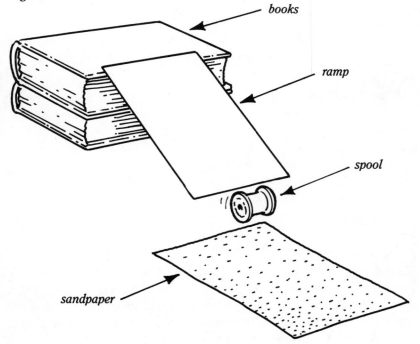

books

ramp

spool

sandpaper

spool, they should replace the fine sandpaper with coarse sandpaper and repeat the experiment. When all the students are finished, have them discuss their observations. Point out that the rolling spool turns toward the sandpaper because the rim that is on the sandpaper slows while the other rim continues to move at its original speed.

AIR-PRESSURE SPOOLS

Problem
Can you blow down on something and not have it fall?

Purpose
To demonstrate low air pressure. To develop skills in experimentation.

What You Need
For each student:
– wood or hard-plastic spool with a single hole
– straight pin
– index card
– scissors

Procedure
Have the students cut a large circle out of the index card—the diameter of the circle should be larger than the diameter of the spool. Tell the students to stick a straight pin through the center of the circle and insert the pin into the hole of the spool.

Tell them to hold the spool with one hand. With one finger of the other hand, they should hold the card in place so it doesn't fall but will allow air to come through the spool. Have them blow *very gently* and steadily through the spool and at the same time bend forward until they are facing and blowing straight down. When in this position, they should remove the finger that holds the card. The card will not fall as long as they continue to blow through the spool.

Ask the students if they can explain why the card does not fall. Discuss their answers. Then explain that the lateral flow of air across the upper surface of the card (especially in that area between the spool and card) is less than the normal force of air pressure. The normal force of air pressure pushing upward under the card keeps the card from falling. (See Figure 13.)

Figure 13

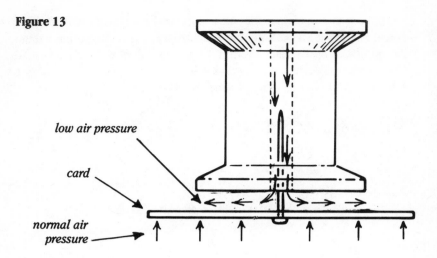

low air pressure

card

normal air pressure

TURNING THE WHEELS

Problem

How can you make wheels turn other wheels?

Purpose

To show cause-and-effect relationships. To develop skills in experimentation and drawing conclusions.

What You Need

For one device:
- 5-10 spools and reels of several sizes and shapes (such as old tape-recorder reels, film reels, and thread spools)
- 5-10 screws
- 5-10 washers
- several long rubber bands
- 60 × 60 cm piece of ½" or ¾" plywood
- screwdriver

Procedure

This device is best used at a learning center. It should be available as long as there is an interest in it and students seem to be learning from it.

To build the device, select five or six of the spools and reels (wheels). Place one or two washers between each wheel and the plywood. Fasten the middle of each wheel securely to the plywood board with a screw. (See Figure 14.) The wheels should turn freely without rubbing against the baseboard. Make a mark on the outer rim of each wheel so revolutions of the wheel can be easily counted.

Figure 14

rubber band   *wheel*   *baseboard*

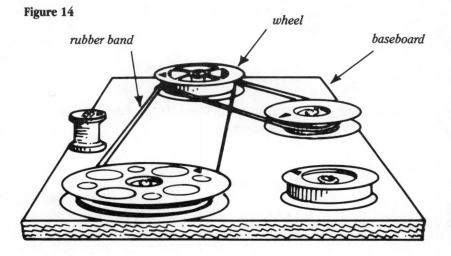

Show students how to connect two or more wheels with the rubber bands. Also show them that all the connected wheels will turn when one of the wheels is turned manually. Caution students not to stretch the rubber bands too tightly—the friction might prevent the wheels from turning. Challenge students to answer questions such as: "If you turn a large wheel that is connected to a small wheel, do both wheels make the same number of revolutions?" "If you turn a small wheel that is connected to a large wheel, do both wheels make the same number of revolutions?" "Can you turn one wheel that makes a second wheel turn in the opposite direction?" "How many rubber bands do you need to make all the wheels on the board turn at the same time?"

You might let older students make up their own challenge problems. A sample problem might be, "Connect two wheels so one wheel makes twice as many turns as the other." Note that students may have to add smaller or larger wheels to do so.

SIMPLE PULLEYS

Purpose

To show how a pulley can be used to lift a load.

What You Need

For the demonstration:
- tape reel (3″ or 5″ plastic reel from an old tape recorder or an 8-mm film reel)
- pencil
- wire coat hanger
- string
- rubber band
- ruler
- weight (between 300 and 500 g—a medium-size textbook works well)
- scissors

Procedure

Before class, construct a simple pulley. To do this bend the wire coat hanger as shown in Figure 15. Hold the tape reel between the two hoops at the bottom of the hanger and stick a pencil through the hoops and the middle of the reel to keep the reel in place. (See Figure 16.) Hang this apparatus on a support. Make sure the reel turns freely.

Cut a piece of string slightly longer than the distance from the reel to the surface below it. Tie the rubber band to one end of the string. Tie

Figure 15

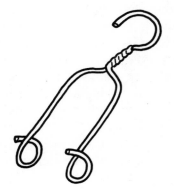

Figure 16

the weight to the other end of the string. Place a paper clip on the rubber band so you can lift the rubber band, string, and weight using the paper clip. When class starts, pull up on the paper clip until the weight is lifted off the work surface. Have a student measure the length of the stretched rubber band and record the measurement. This measurement gives a rough indication of the weight of the load being lifted.

Next, place the string into the groove of the pulley wheel, so you can pull down on the paper clip to lift the weight. (See Figure 17.) Make sure that the weight and the string can move freely without rubbing against anything.

Figure 17

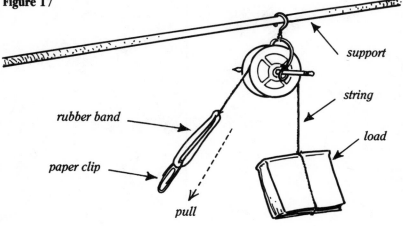

support

string

rubber band

load

paper clip

pull

Pull down on the string to lift the load. Have another student measure the length of the stretched rubber band. Record the results. Then ask students when the rubber band stretched more.

Explain that the apparatus you are using is called a *single fixed pulley*. This type of pulley does not give the user any mechanical advantage. That is, you need at least 1000 g of force pulling downward to lift a load of 1000 g upward. However, the single fixed pulley is useful because it changes the direction of the force. You can lift a weight up by pulling down.

Tell students that you can make another type of simple pulley using the same materials. Remove the weight from the string and remove the pulley from the support. Tie the free end of the string to the support. Tie another piece of string around the weight. Turn the pulley wheel upside down so the weight can hang from the pulley hook. Run the string under the pulley and attach the weight to the pulley hanger. (See Figure 18.)

Figure 18

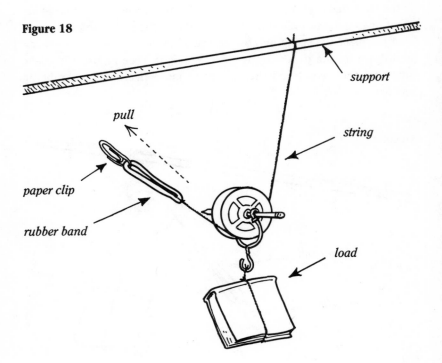

Pull upward until the load is lifted off the work surface. Have a student measure the length of the rubber band and record the measurement. Ask the students if the rubber band is stretched more or less than when you used the single fixed pulley. Point out that even though you are lifting the weight *and* the pulley, less force is needed to lift the weight. Ask students if they can explain this occurrence.

Explain that this type of pulley is called a *single movable pulley*. A single movable pulley makes it easier to lift a load because it distributes the weight of the load at two points—the point where the string is attached to the support and the point where the force is being applied (the other end of the string).

6

EXPERIENCES WITH BOXES

Children seem drawn to boxes. These everyday objects appear to invite play, exploration, and imaginative activities that range from simply crawling into a box to elaborate box constructions. You can use boxes to stimulate curiosity, invite investigation, and develop science skills while revealing basic scientific laws, theories, and facts.

In this chapter, boxes are used in experiments that allow students to explore and probe an unknown and unseen object, to discover a property of light, and to interact with levers.

PROBING A "MYSTERY" BOX

Problem

What can probes teach you about a hidden object?

Purpose

To develop skills in observation, recording data, and hypothesizing.

What You Need

For each group of four or five students:
- shoe box
- object to be placed in box (such as a brick, a large stone, a block of wood, a sponge, a smaller box, or any other large, unbreakable object)
- masking tape or package tape
- stiff wire probe, 2 cm longer than the shoe box (A thin knitting needle or a slightly sharpened section of a wire coat hanger works well.)

Procedure

Before class prepare one "mystery" box for each group of students. Put an object in each shoe box and tape the object down so it will not slide or roll. (Each box should contain a different object.) Place the covers on the boxes and tape them securely in place.

At class time, announce that students will do an investigation to learn about limitations that scientists must sometimes deal with. Explain that each group's task is to draw the object in their box. Emphasize that they should not try to identify or name the object.

Next, tell the class that they have to work under limiting conditions. Write the following directions on the chalkboard and leave them there throughout the experiment:

1. Do not open the box or peek into it.
2. Do not lift, turn, or rotate the box—it must remain in place on the desk or table.
3. Only the wire probe may be used to obtain data.
4. The probe can be pushed through the sides or top of the box. However, the probe must form a right angle with the surface of the box.
5. When the probe strikes the object, the probe must not be pushed any further, wriggled, or tapped.
6. The picture must be drawn after twenty-five probes.

Before students start the experiment, it might be necessary to suggest that they devise some way to record their observations. Let them create their own methods.

Have the class test the boxes, watching carefully to make sure they follow the directions. After each group has completed its drawing, permit the students to open the box and compare the object inside with the drawing. They should also be given the opportunity to move about the room and look at other group's drawings.

Discuss the difficulties students had with the experiment. Point out that the limitations made it very difficult to accurately draw the object. Ask questions such as: "What limitations do scientists who study atoms and molecules experience?" "What limitations do doctors of internal medicine and neurosurgeons experience?" "What limitations do astronomers experience?"

Students should conclude from the experiment and the discussion that scientists often work with limitations imposed on them. They are limited by the capabilities and precision of their instruments, and by current knowledge. As more knowledge and better instruments become available, ideas about the world change.

A PUZZLE BOX

Problem

Can you draw a picture of an unseen mechanism by observing only its input and output actions?

Purpose

To develop skills in observation, prediction, and experimentation.

What You Need

For each puzzle box:
- cardboard box (preferably 20 × 20 × 40 cm)
- 4 pieces of corrugated cardboard (10 cm wide and as long as the length of the box)
- ¼"-diameter dowel (as long as the width of the box)
- ruler or board of similar size (30 cm long)
- glue
- yarn (2 colors)
- 8 large steel washers (5 cm diameter)
- drill
- scissors
- 6-8 textbooks

Procedure

This device is best used at a learning center. It should be available as long as there is an interest in it and students seem to be learning from it.

To build the puzzle box, glue the cardboard strips together in pairs. When the glue is dry, cut "v" notches in the center of each strip. Cut another notch on each side of the center notch as shown in Figure 19. Glue each strip inside the box against a long side of the box. The bottoms of the strips should rest against the bottom of the box. (See Figure 20.) Cut a slit in the bottom of the box. The opening should be 5 mm wide and 30 cm long.

Figure 19

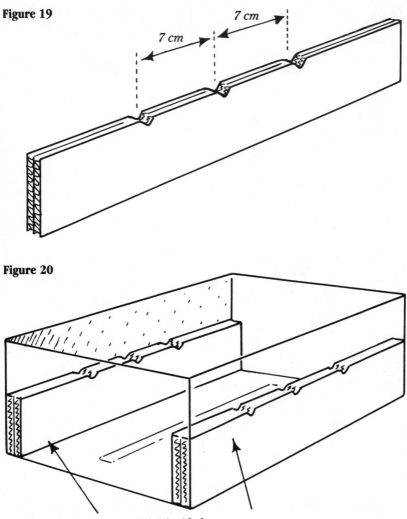

Figure 20

strips inside box

Starting 5 cm away from the edge of the ruler, drill five ¼″ holes spaced 5 cm apart. (See Figure 21.) Slide the dowel through the center hole in the ruler. Tie a piece of yarn through the holes at each end of the ruler. Use a different color of yarn on each side. Tie three or four washers to each piece of yarn. (See Figure 22.)

Figure 21

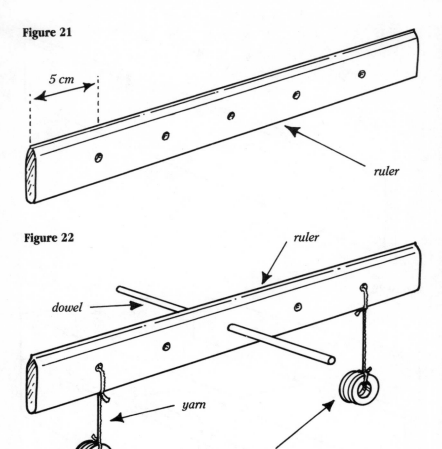

5 cm

ruler

Figure 22

ruler

dowel

yarn

3 or 4 washers

Rest the ends of the dowel in the center notches of the cardboard strips. Push the washers and yarn through the bottom slit so they hang out of the bottom of the box. Lightly tape down the cover of the box.

When class starts, show students the closed box. Show them that when you pull down on one set of washers, the other washers move up. Place the box on top of two equal stacks of books so the weights can be freely manipulated. (See Figure 23.) Then challenge the students to draw a picture of the mechanism inside the box.

Figure 23

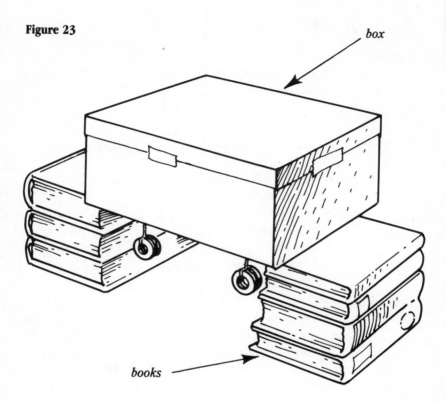

box

books

Let students play with the box for several days. Then open the box and let students compare their drawings with the mechanism.

You can create other puzzle challenges by changing the position of the washers or dowel (or both). Some samples include:

1. Moving the dowel to a different hole, leaving the washers in their original positions.
2. Moving one set of washers to a different hole, leaving the other washers and the dowel in their original positions.

This activity can be used to introduce levers and cause-and-effect relationships. It can also be used to develop skills in observation and experimentation.

PATHS OF LIGHT

Purpose

To show that mirrors can be used to change the path of a light beam.

What You Need

For the demonstration:
— box with lid (preferably a flat box such as a business envelope box)
— 4 blocks of wood (at least 3 × 3 × 5 cm)
— 4 small mirrors
— black construction paper
— waxed paper
— flashlight
— scissors
— glue or tape

Procedure

Before class, cut a 2 × 2 cm window in one end of the box. Cut three more windows—one in the center and the others near the corners—in the opposite end of the box. (See Figure 24.) Tape several layers of waxed paper over the three windows. Line the box with construction paper, leaving the windows open. Glue or tape each mirror to a block of wood.

Figure 24

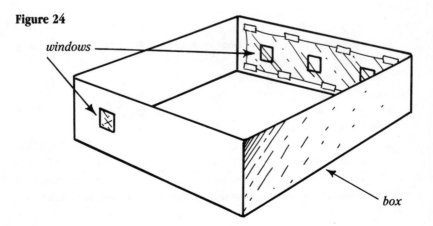

windows

box

Using the flashlight, a protractor, and a flat mirror, show students that light reflects from a mirror at the same angle that the light reaches the mirror. Once students understand this concept, place the flashlight near the box so light shines into the single window. (The three-window end of the box should face the class.) Arrange two mirrors so the light beam can be seen through only one window at the opposite end of the box. (See Figure 25.) Darken the room so the effect is visible.

Figure 25

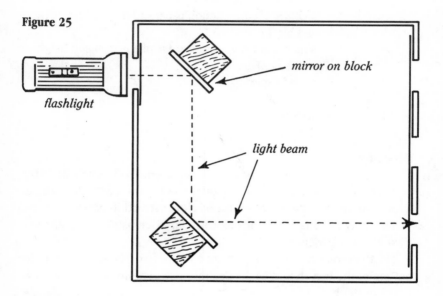

flashlight

mirror on block

light beam

Challenge the students to draw a possible arrangement of mirrors that would produce the observed results. Then rearrange the mirrors so the light shines through a different window. You can also change the number of mirrors you use. Challenge the students to draw the new configuration.

To extend this experiment, use large mirrors in a darkened classroom. Have two or three students hold the mirrors and one student hold a flashlight. Challenge the students to bounce the beam of light off all the mirrors onto some object in the classroom. (You might want to use concave mirrors, which will keep the light beam from spreading each time it is reflected.)

REFLECTED COLORS

Purpose

To show that light reflected from a colored surface will have the color of that surface.

What You Need

For the demonstration:
— box with a cover (at least 30 cm long and 20 cm high)
— 5 colors of construction paper (3 bright colors, white, and black)
— 4 pieces of heavy cardboard (same length and height as the box)
— waxed paper
— tape or glue
— scissors
— flashlight

Procedure

Before class, cut an elongated window in one side of the box. The window should be 4 cm from the bottom of the box and at least 5 cm high. Line the box with black construction paper or, if you prefer, spray the interior of the box with flat black paint. Make sure you leave the window open.

Use the cardboard to make partitions in the box. The window and the bottom of the box should be divided into five sections. Fasten the cardboard to the bottom of the box with tape. Cut rectangles from the five colors of construction paper and place them in the box between the partitions. (There should be one color in each section.) Cover the window with several layers of waxed paper. (See Figure 26.)

Place the box on a table or desk with the window facing the class. Darken the room and hold the flashlight so the beam of light shines on only one of the brightly colored pieces of paper. Ask students to look at the window and guess which color paper the light is falling on. (The color should be visible in the window above the paper.) Move the flashlight so it shines on another color and repeat the question. Continue with the third color, and the white and black sections. (White or rather colorless light will be seen above the white paper. Little or no light will be seen above the black paper.)

Figure 26

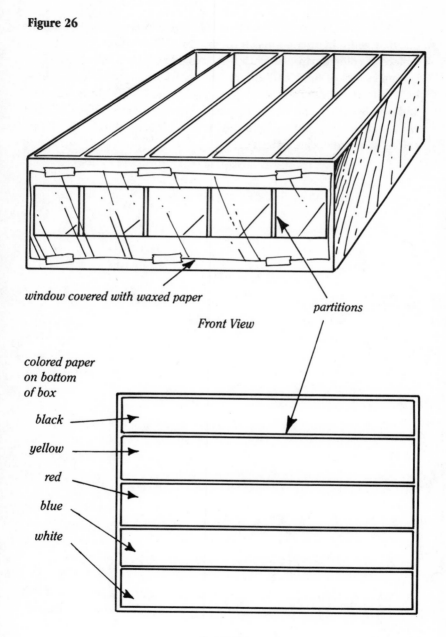

window covered with waxed paper

partitions

Front View

colored paper
on bottom
of box

black

yellow

red

blue

white

Top View

Ask the class if they can explain why this experiment works. Point out that white light contains all the colors. If white light is directed at a piece of colored paper or cloth, the colored pigments will reflect only certain colors of light and absorb the rest. For example, when white light falls on a green carpet, the green part of the white light is reflected and all the other colors are absorbed. White surfaces reflect all the colors, so white light is reflected. Black surfaces absorb all of the colors, so no colors are reflected.

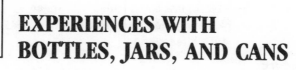

7 EXPERIENCES WITH BOTTLES, JARS, AND CANS

Ask students to bring in bottles, jars, and cans, and you will soon have more than enough for these experiments and demonstrations. Glass bottles of several shapes are useful in the light experiments. Salad-dressing bottles are suggested, though cologne, perfume, and wine bottles also work well. Avoid using bottles with raised or indented markings, as these will distort light rays. Coffee cans and soup cans for the friction and center-of-mass experiments should be clean inside and out. Make sure the labels are removed and there are no sharp edges before using the cans.

MIXING COLORED LIGHT

Problem

What happens when two different colors of light fall on the same surface?

Purpose

To show that different colors of light can be combined to make other colors. To develop skills in observation, prediction, and drawing conclusions.

What You Need

For each group of four students:
- 3-4 clear glass bottles with relatively flat sides filled with water (Bottles should not have impressed images.)
- flashlight or similar bright light source
- food coloring (red, blue, yellow, and green)
- crayons (red, blue, yellow, and green)
- stiff white tagboard
- white drawing paper

For the demonstration:
- 2 clear glass bottles filled with water
- blue and yellow food coloring
- stiff white tagboard

Procedure

Start the class with a demonstration. Drop three to five drops of blue coloring in the first bottle and stir well. Drop three to five drops of yellow coloring in the second bottle and stir well. Fold the tagboard so it can stand by itself. (See Figure 27.)

Figure 27

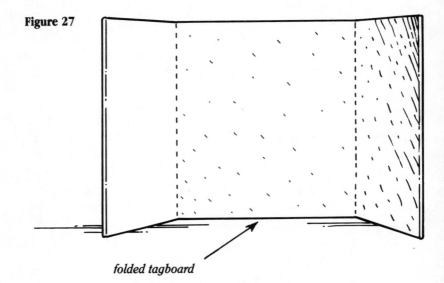

folded tagboard

Place the bottle of blue water about 10 cm in front of the tagboard "screen." Turn on the flashlight and direct the light beam on the bottle so the light passes through the colored water and falls on the screen. Have students observe the color that appears on the screen (blue). Repeat using the yellow water. Then ask students to guess what would happen if the light passed through both bottles. Try it. Then have students use crayons to mix blue and yellow on a sheet of white paper. Ask the students if mixing the crayon colors produced the same results as mixing the light colors.

Hand out the materials so students can experiment with different color combinations. Have students keep a record that shows the color combinations they tried, their predicted results, and their actual results. Also ask them to see if mixing the colors with crayons produces the same results. (Mixing pigment colors will produce some results that are different than the same combination with light. This occurs because the primary colors of pigments are red, yellow, and blue while the primary colors of light are red, green, and blue.)

OBSERVING LIGHT RAYS

Purpose

To show that light rays can be observed.

What You Need

For the demonstration:
- several clear glass jars that are similar in size and shape (such as mayonnaise jars)
- shoe box or similar box
- flashlight
- aluminum foil
- tape
- pin or needle
- pitcher of water
- milk
- substances to add to water (such as food coloring, gelatin powder, chalk dust, detergent, and so on)

Procedure

Cut a 3 × 3 cm opening in one end of the shoe box. In the other end of the box, cut an opening large enough for the flashlight head. Tape a piece of aluminum foil over the square opening. Use a pin or needle to carefully punch four holes in the foil. The holes should be in a vertical line and about 1 mm apart.

Fill the jar with water. Stir in about two teaspoons of milk. If necessary, add more milk until the solution is murky. Place the head of the flashlight into the box. Align the jar of milky water with the foil-covered opening. Darken the room and turn on the flashlight. Light should shine through the holes in the foil. Move the jar back and forth until four distinct rays of light can be seen in the water solution.

Ask students if they can guess why the light rays became visible. Then experiment with other materials to see if they support the students' predictions. Use fresh jars of water and solutions made with things such as food coloring, gelatin powder, and chalk dust.

After you have spent some time experimenting, explain that light rays can be observed when they strike particles suspended in a solution or in the air. For instance, this phenomenon occurs when the sun is low in the sky and light clouds are present. The sun's rays strike moisture droplets and dust or smoke particles in the air. Another example is a light beam from a projector that becomes visible when dust is stirred up in the room.

If you wish, you can extend this demonstration to include lenses. After you have set up the flashlight and the jar of solution, place a lens between the shoe box and the jar. Have the class observe how the lens causes the light rays to converge or diverge. Use different lenses to show different effects.

MAKING A LENS OUT OF WATER

Problem

How can water act as a lens?

Purpose

To develop skills in experimentation and manipulation of materials.

What you need

For each group of four to six students:
— 4-8 clear glass bottles, jars, and vials of several sizes and shapes (Make sure there are no images on the glass.)
— shoe box
— scissors
— flashlight
— aluminum foil
— tape

- stiff white tagboard
- pitcher of water
- pin or needle

Procedure

Discuss lenses and magnifying glasses with the class. Point out that many magnifying lenses are thick in the center and thin at the edges. Tell students that they will be trying to make water act like a lens.

Hand out the materials and have each group cut out a 3 × 3 cm opening in one end of the shoe box. Then have them cut out an opening large enough to admit the head of a flashlight in the other end of the box. A piece of aluminum foil should be taped over the square opening. Have students use a pin or needle to punch four small holes in the foil. The holes should be in a horizontal line and no more than 1 mm apart. (See Figure 28.)

Figure 28

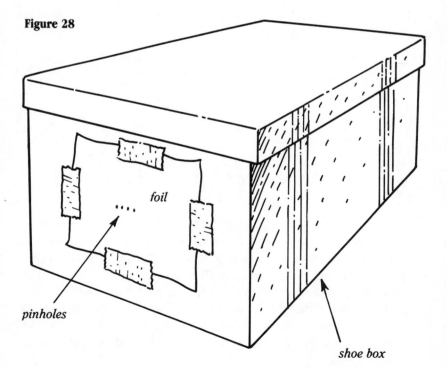

foil

pinholes

shoe box

Have each group place a flashlight in the large opening and turn the light on. Light should shine through the pinholes in the foil. Have the students fold the white tagboard so it can stand by itself. Tell the students to place the tagboard "screen" in front of the light beams. Have each group place one of the bottles between the foil-covered opening and the screen. (See Figure 29.) Darken the room.

Figure 29

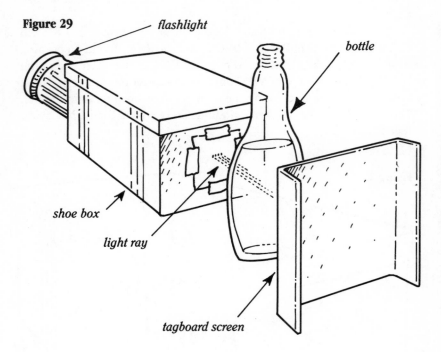

flashlight

bottle

shoe box

light ray

tagboard screen

Walk around the room and check that the light rays pass through the bottle and are visible as distinct points on the screen. If they are not, reposition the bottle until distinct points appear. After you have checked each group's work, have them carefully pour water into the bottles. Tell the students to observe and record what happens to the points on the screen. Point out that there may be differences in the size and location of the light points. Have the students test other bottles and jars and record their results. Make sure they align each bottle properly before filling it with water.

After students have finished experimenting, turn on the light and discuss their results. You might ask them questions such as: "Which bottles made the light beams converge?" "Which bottles made the light beams diverge?" "Did the size of the bottle make a difference?" "Did the shape of the bottle make a difference?"

Explain that light rays do not bend very much when they pass through a glass bottle. However, if water is added to the bottle, the water takes on the shape of the bottle, which is basically that of a lens. The water "lens" bends the light rays in the same way a glass lens would. You might want to point out that bottles of clear liquids that are carelessly thrown onto dry grass or leaves have been known to start fires. The bottle of liquid acts as a lens and focuses the sun's rays on a small area. This heats the dry material and causes it to ignite.

THE HEAT OF FRICTION

Problem

How can we show that friction produces heat?

Purpose

To show that mechanical energy can be changed into heat energy. To develop skills in observation and recording data.

What You Need

For each group of three or four students:
— coffee can with snap-on lid
— several cups of sand or fine gravel (should be at room temperature)
— thermometer

Procedure

Start the experiment by discussing friction and its effects. Point out that friction occurs when one surface rubs against another. Also mention that friction produces heat, though sometimes the amount of heat produced is not observable.

Hand out the materials. Have each group fill a coffee can halfway with sand or gravel. Tell the students to push the thermometer bulb into the sand so the bulb is covered and to leave it there for at least thirty seconds. Have each group read their thermometer and record the temperature of the sand.

Now have the students remove the thermometer and put the lid on the can. Have one student in each group pick up the can and shake it vigorously for at least thirty seconds. When the students are done, they should set the can down, lift off the lid, and insert the thermometer for at least thirty seconds. Have the students read and record the temperature. Allow each student in the group to repeat the procedure.

Discuss the results with the students. Ask them if they know where the heat came from. Point out that mechanical energy is used to shake the can. As the students shake the can, grains of sand rub against each other and against the inside surface of the can. This friction produces heat. The observed temperature change indicates the amount of mechanical energy that was converted into heat energy.

A LOPSIDED CAN

Purpose

To show that changing the center of gravity can influence the behavior of a rolling can.

What You Need

For the demonstration:
- metal can with lid
- cardboard
- masking tape
- scissors

For each student (optional):
- metal can with lid
- cardboard
- masking tape
- scissors

Procedure

Before class make a "lopsided" can. Cut a piece of cardboard so its length is the same as the can's length and its width is 1.5 cm greater than the diameter of the can. Bend or curl the cardboard just enough so it can be slid into the can. Insert the cardboard, and then stick a piece of masking tape on the outside of the can opposite the concave bend of the cardboard. (See Figure 30.) Put on the lid.

Figure 30

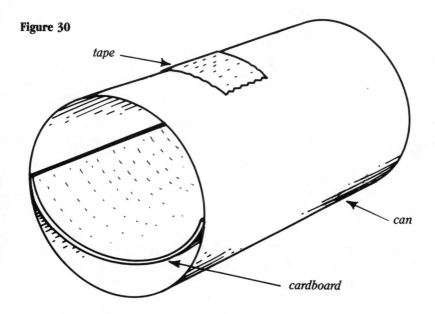

tape

can

cardboard

Show students how the can works. Roll it on a smooth surface such as a tabletop or tiled floor. The can will always stop with the tape on top. Ask a student to move the tape to a new spot on the outside of the can. Tell the class you will now make the can perform the same trick. Lift the lid (in such a way that students cannot see the inside of the can) and rotate the cardboard until the concave surface is once again opposite the tape. Replace the lid and roll the can.

Repeat this several times, and then tell the students that all you have inside the can is a piece of cardboard. Challenge them to tell you how the can works. (If you wish, have students try to make cans that behave in the same way.)

After a set amount of time, show the students how your can was made. Explain that the bent cardboard inside the can shifts the center of gravity (or center of mass) to one side of the can. The "heavy" side moves when you move the cardboard.

BALANCING ACT

Purpose

To demonstrate the center of mass.

What You Need

For the demonstration:
— metal can (10–12 cm high)
— piece of stiff, heavy wire (at least 3½ times longer than the height of the can)
— masking tape
— 6–8 pencils of different lengths
— metal washers, fishing sinkers, or Plasticine (Total weight must be slightly more than the weight of the can.)
— pliers

Procedure

Before class make a can that can be balanced over the edge of a table or desktop. This is done as follows: Bend about 2 cm of one end of the wire into a candy-cane shape over the top of the can. Then use tape to fasten the wire against the side of the can. Now bend the other end of the wire into a "j" shape. Bend the whole loose end of the wire into a gentle curve so the lower end of the wire is beyond the opposite rim of the can. (See Figure 31.)

Place the pencils in the can. Attach the washers, sinkers, or Plasticine to the bottom end of the wire. Then set the can on the edge of a table or desk as shown in Figure 32. Only a third or fourth of the can's bottom should rest on the table. (You may have to adjust the weights or wire slightly.) The weights must be beyond the edge of the can.

When students enter the class, point out the balancing can. Ask the class what they think will happen if the pencils were removed. They will probably guess that the can will fall off the table.

Once the students' curiosities have been aroused, slowly and carefully remove one pencil at a time from the can. When all the pencils have been removed, challenge students to explain why the can is still balanced on the table. If they suggest that the weights at the end of the wire are responsible, remove one weight at a time until the can falls.

Explain that when the weights were added to the lower end of the wire, the center of the total mass of the objects (can, wire, and weights) moved to a point near the edge of the can. When the weights are removed, the center of mass changes, and the can falls.

Figure 31

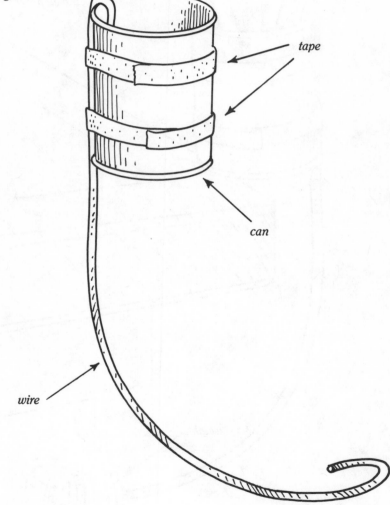

tape

can

wire

Figure 32

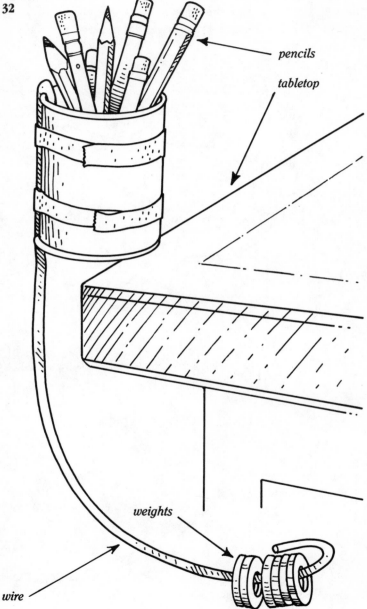

pencils

tabletop

weights

wire

8

EXPERIENCES WITH MARBLES

Marbles and balls are used as playthings in many cultures around the world. It is not surprising, therefore, that children are attracted to and challenged by science activities that involve marbles.

The experiences in this chapter focus on motion and the forces that affect motion. The science concepts involved are relatively simple concepts—they help explain things that we experience every day.

AFFECTING FRICTION

Problem

Do variations in surface texture affect friction?

Purpose

To show that different surface textures produce different amounts of friction. To develop skills in manipulation of controls and variables.

What You Need

For each group of three or four students:
— marble
— "channel" such as an angled piece of iron (30 cm long)
— 3-4 carpet samples with different types of pile (such as shag carpet, kitchen carpet, and short-loop carpet)
— piece of wood or several books (needs to be 8 cm high)

Procedure

Arrange the channel and the wood or books as shown in Figure 33. The lower end of the channel should rest on the desk.

Figure 33

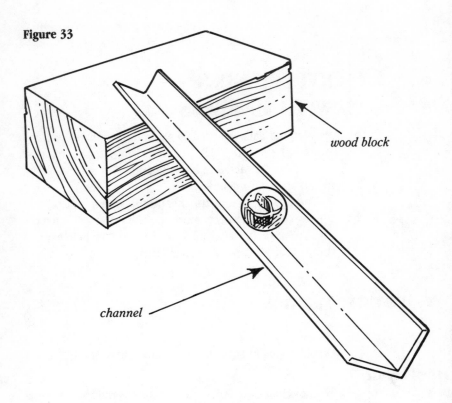

wood block

channel

Hold the marble in the channel near the top and ask the students to guess what will happen when you release the marble. They will probably say that the marble will roll down the channel and across the desk. Release the marble and have the students observe the motion. Then ask them if the marble would roll as far if the surface of the desk were very rough.

Hand out the materials to each group. Tell the students they will use the materials to see if changes in surface texture affect the distance a marble rolls.

Have students set up the channel so the lower end of the channel rests on a carpet sample. Explain that the students should start the marble at the same point for each test and let it roll until it stops. Once the marble has stopped, students should measure and record the distance from the low end of the channel to the marble. Have students test each carpet sample three times. When they have finished, they should calculate the average distance the marble rolled for each sample. Also mention that if the marble rolls off the end of the sample, students should use a lower starting point for *each* test.

Students' results will show that some types of carpet slow the marble very quickly. Thick or soft pile carpets produce more friction and absorb the marble's energy. Thin or "harder" carpets are smoother so they produce less friction.

Discuss the results with the class. You should also encourage a discussion about controls and variables. Ask questions such as, "Why is it important to use the same marble for each test?" and "Why was it important to start the marble at the same place each time?"

A MARBLE CANNON

Purpose

To demonstrate Newton's third law of motion—for every action there is an equal and opposite reaction.

What You Need

For the demonstation:
- 12 or more marbles of the same size
- 1-2 larger marbles
- wood board (10 × 18 cm)
- several rubber bands of different widths
- 3 nails (at least 5 cm long)
- string
- scissors
- hammer

Procedure

Before class prepare the "cannon." Hammer the nails into the top of the board as shown in Figure 34. The nails should stick up at least 4 cm. Place a rubber band around the two nails near the edge of the board. Tie a piece of string around the middle of the rubber band. Then pull the string back toward the third nail until the rubber band is stretched back at least 3 cm. Tie the string securely to the third nail. The board should now look like Figure 35.

Figure 34

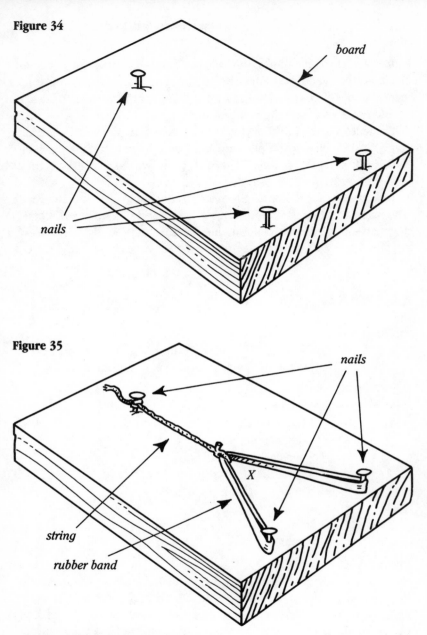

board

nails

Figure 35

nails

string

rubber band

X

Marble will be placed at point X.

When class starts, begin a discussion by asking students if they skate (either roller-skating or ice-skating). Have them imagine two skaters facing each other with their hands together. Ask the class what would happen if the skaters pushed against each other. (The skaters would move apart.) Then ask what would happen if both skaters faced in the same direction and one pushed against the other's back. If students say that both skaters would move, you should encourage them to think about how far the skaters would move and if the size and weight of the skaters would make a difference in the distance.

Now invite the class to watch the demonstration closely and to think about how it relates to the questions about the skaters.

Take the marbles of the same size and lay them on a smooth table in the pattern shown in Figure 36. Place the board over four or six of the marbles. Then place another marble at the "X" intersection on the board. (See Figure 35.)

Figure 36

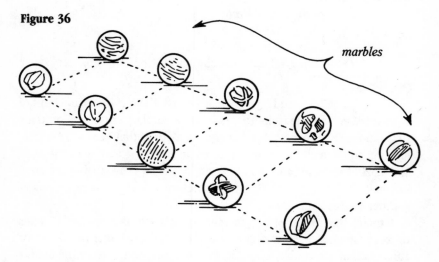

marbles

Make sure students are not standing too close to the table. Cut the string right next to the third nail. The marble, propelled by the rubber band, will fly in one direction while the board rolls in the opposite direction. Replace the string and repeat the demonstration. (Make sure you use the same marble and have the same amount of stretch on the rubber band.) Note how far the marble is thrown and how far the board moves. Explain that students have seen an example of Newton's third law of motion—for every action there is an equal and opposite reaction. (At this point students may argue that the cannon did not move as far as the marble. Point out that the board is heavier than the marble. Ask them what would happen if a very light skater and a very heavy skater pushed against each other.)

You can repeat this demonstration as many times as you wish. You might try using different-sized marbles, different rubber band widths, and different amounts of stretch on the rubber band.

CIRCULAR MOTION

Purpose

To demonstrate inertia and centripetal force.

What You Need

For the demonstration:
— large marble
— circular mixing bowl
— Ping-Pong ball or similar ball (optional)

Procedure

Show students the marble. Ask them if they can think of a way to get the marble to move in a circle. Try some of their suggestions. If students do not suggest a method that keeps the marble moving, show them the following method: Place the marble in the bowl and make it move around the upper rim of the bowl by moving the bowl in small circles. If you wish, you can repeat this demonstration using another type of ball.

Explain that when you push something, such as a marble, it tends to keep moving in a straight line. This is called *inertia*. To show students that the marble rolling in the bowl has inertia, place the marble on a table and place the bowl over it. Move the bowl in fast, small circles until you can hear the marble moving around the edge of the bowl. Then lift the bowl—the marble will move across the table in a straight line.

Tell students that the marble moves in a circle in the bowl because the effect of its inertia is balanced by an inward force. This force is known as *centripetal force*. In this demonstration, the centripetal force is the force of the bowl on the marble. The bowl "pushes" on the marble, keeping it in a circular path.

Mention that we experience these forces almost every day. For example, when a car turns a corner, the passengers tend to sway or lean away from the curve. The passengers are experiencing inertia—they want to keep going in a straight line. However, the car exerts centripetal force on the passengers—it forces them to turn the corner.

STICKY LIQUIDS

Purpose

To show that different liquids have different viscosities.

What You Need

For the demonstration:
- 4 marbles of the same size
- 4 test tubes or similar flasks
- water (enough to fill 1 test tube)
- cooking oil (enough to fill 1 test tube)
- honey or clear syrup (enough to fill 1 test tube)
- thick, clear shampoo (enough to fill 1 test tube)

Procedure

Ask students if they can explain why some liquids pour quickly and others pour slowly. Explain that the *viscosity* of a liquid causes it to resist flowing (or pouring). Liquids with a high viscosity pour slowly and are usually fairly thick, while liquids with a low viscosity pour quickly and are usually fairly thin.

Fill each test tube with a different liquid. Ask students to guess which liquids have a high viscosity and which liquids have a low viscosity. Write the students' predictions on the chalkboard.

Select four students to help you with the experiment. Have each student hold a marble over the mouth of a test tube. Tell the helpers that they should drop the marbles into the tubes when you say "go." The rest of the class should observe the speed of the marbles as they fall.

Say, "One, two, three, go!" Students will be able to see the different speeds of the marbles in different liquids. Ask students to relate the speed of the marble falling through the liquid to the viscosity of the liquid. (A slowly falling marble indicates a higher viscosity. A quickly falling marble indicates a lower viscosity.) Have students compare the results of the demonstration to their predictions.

Explain that viscosity is caused by the internal friction of the liquid's molecules moving against one another. The more strongly a fluid's molecules interact, the more viscous the fluid. Ask students to think of some highly viscous liquids that are useful.

9 EXPERIENCES WITH PAPER AND PLASTIC CUPS

A huge variety of disposable cups is available today. Small paper cups are used in hospitals to distribute medicines. Tiny paper cups are used in the fast-food industry to serve mustard and catsup. Coffee, soft drinks, and milkshakes are served in many different sizes of paper, hard plastic, and Styrofoam cups. Clear plastic beverage cups are frequently used at parties and social gatherings.

Many of these cups can be used to teach important science lessons. Some of the activities call for paper cups, some call for hard plastic cups, and some call for Styrofoam cups. Be sure to get the kind of cup recommended for each activity.

OBSERVING DRIPS

Problem

Will different liquids drip through a hole at the same rate?

Purpose

To show that different liquids have different viscosities. To develop skills in observation, experimentation, recording data, and drawing conclusions.

What You Need

For each group of four students:
- 8 plastic or Styrofoam cups
- 8 Popsicle sticks or similar sticks
- 4 liquids with different viscosities (such as water, whole milk, cooking oil, liquid detergent, catsup, or shampoo)
- small nail or brad

Procedure

Have students use a small nail or brad to poke a hole in the bottom of four cups. Make sure the holes are the same size—students should not wiggle the nail while punching the hole. Tell students to place two Popsicle sticks across the top of each remaining cup. They should set the cups with holes on top of the sticks so each hole is between the sticks and is free to drain. (See Figure 37.)

Figure 37

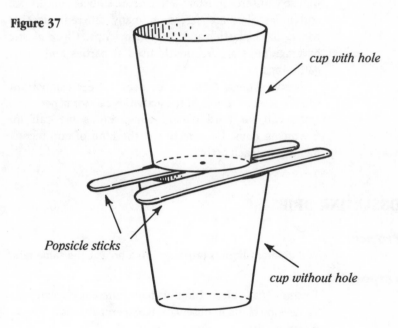

cup with hole

Popsicle sticks

cup without hole

Tell students to pour a different liquid into each top cup. They should put the same amount of liquid into each cup, and they should record the time when each liquid is poured into a cup. Have students observe the cups every five minutes. They should record the number of five-minute intervals it takes for each cup to drain. Once all the cups have drained, each group should make a graph of its results (liquid versus time).

After the graphs are made, have the students dip a finger into each liquid and rub the liquid between the thumb and finger. Ask them to relate the stickiness of each liquid with the speed the liquid drains through the hole. (Thick, sticky liquids drain through the hole slowly, while thin liquids drain through the hole more quickly.) Point out that the "stickiness" of a liquid is called *viscosity*.

You can also have students do an extension of this experiment using a syrup-water solution. Have the students set up two sets of cups as before. Make a solution of half syrup and half water. Have the students pour 100 ml of pure syrup into one top cup and 100 ml of the syrup solution into the other top cup. Have students predict which cup will drain more slowly.

INSULATING CUPS

Problem

Do Styrofoam cups really keep cold liquids cold and hot liquids hot?

Purpose

To show that Styrofoam cups are insulators.

What You Need

For each pair of students:
- plastic cup
- Styrofoam cup
- 2 plastic containers (such as margarine tubs or cottage cheese containers)
- 2 thermometers
- ice cubes
- hot water
- cold water
- measuring cup or beaker

Procedure

Ask students if they know what a thermal insulator is. Explain that an insulator can keep hot things hot, and cold things cold. Ask if students think Styrofoam cups are insulators. Tell the class that they will be testing Styrofoam to see if it really is an insulator.

Hand out the materials. Have students pour 240 ml of hot water into each plastic container. Then have them pour 240 ml of cold water into the plastic cup and the Styrofoam cup. Students should place an ice cube in each cup and then set each cup into a container of hot water. (Point out that the ice cubes should be the same size.)

Have students observe the ice cubes and compare the time it takes for the cubes in the two cups to melt. (Students will discover that the ice cube in the Styrofoam cup melts more slowly, which proves Styrofoam cups help keep liquids cold.)

Have students repeat the experiment, using ice water in the containers and hot water in the cups. They should measure the initial temperature of the hot water in both cups, and then measure the temperature again ten minutes later. (The water in the plastic cup will be cooler, which shows Styrofoam cups help keep liquids warm.)

TO RUST OR NOT TO RUST?

Problem

What substances can make iron rust more quickly?

Purpose

To show that some household substances promote the rusting of iron. To develop skills in observation and collection of data.

What You Need

For each group of two to four students:
— 4 clear plastic cups
— 4 iron nails (not galvanized)
— 4 different household substances (such as oil, liquid detergent, glass cleaner, rubbing alcohol, soda pop, vanilla extract, lemon or lime juice, vinegar, salt, or baking soda) CAUTION! Do not use toilet bowl cleaners, drain openers, or lye. These are very caustic and can cause serious burns.
— aluminum foil
— string
— plastic wrap
— shoe box or cake pan
— scissors

Procedure

Ask students if they can think of a way to prevent iron from rusting. Point out that most iron objects are covered or coated with a material to prevent rusting. Then ask students if they know of any substances that might make iron rust more quickly.

Place an iron nail in a plastic cup and cover it with plastic wrap. Explain that this nail will be used as the control. Have students tie a piece of string to each of the remaining nails. They should place each nail in a separate cup with the string hanging over the top of the cup. Tell students they should use the string to remove the nail from the liquid in the cup. Have the students pour one substance into each cup. The liquid should cover the nail. If students are using dry or powdered substances, they should add ½ teaspoon of the substance to the cup and then add enough water to cover the nail. Students should cover the cups with plastic wrap.

Have students place the cups in a foil-lined shoe box or cake pan in case any liquid leaks through the cups. Each group should inspect the nails once a day for five days. If no rust appears, let the cups stand for five more days. Have students make a chart that shows which substances promoted rust and how many days elasped before the rust appeared. Make sure they compare the nails in the solution with the control nail.

Explain that iron combines with oxygen in the presence of moisture to form rust. The reaction is called *oxidation.* Some chemicals allow the iron and oxygen to react, while others shield the iron from the oxygen. Ask students which substances appear to allow the iron and oxygen to react and which appear to shield the iron from the oxygen.

Note: When cleaning up after this experiment, make sure the substances are poured down the drain one at a time and the drain is rinsed thoroughly with water before the next substance is poured. This prevents dangerous chemical reactions from occurring in the drain.

DANCING SALT

Purpose

To show that sound and vibration are related, and to show that the loudness of a sound and the amount of vibration are related.

What You Need

For the demonstration:
- paper cup
- scissors
- clear plastic wrap
- rubber band
- salt
- working portable radio with flat, built-in speaker

Procedure

Show students that vibration causes sound. Place some salt on a table and hit the table. Ask students if the salt moved when the sound occurred.

Cut off the bottom of the paper cup, being careful not to crush the sides. Stretch a small piece of plastic wrap over the open cup bottom and fasten it in place with a rubber band. Show students the radio. Point out that the sound comes out of the speaker. Find a music station and then turn off the radio. Place the radio on the desk so the speaker faces up. Place the top of the cup on the speaker and sprinkle a few grains of salt on the plastic wrap. (See Figure 38.)

Figure 38

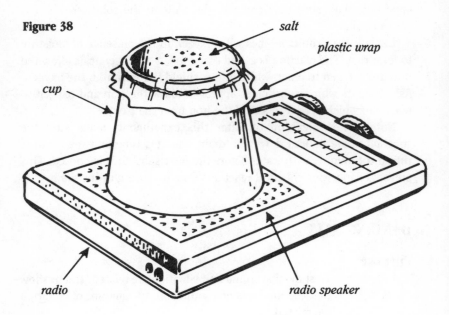

salt

plastic wrap

cup

radio

radio speaker

Gently turn on the radio, keeping the volume very low. Ask students to observe the salt grains. Then *slowly* turn up the volume, being very careful not to jiggle the radio. Ask students whether the salt grains move more or less when the volume is higher. (The louder the volume, the greater the motion of the salt.)

Move the cup off the radio and find a new station that has a talk show or a news broadcast. Place the radio back on the table and place the cup on the radio again. (You may need to sprinkle a few more grains of salt on the plastic.) Have the students observe the salt carefully for a minute or two. They may notice that words that start with "p," "d," or "b" cause the salt to move more than words that begin with "h," "e," or "a."

Explain that parts of the speaker vibrate to produce the sound we hear. When the cup is placed over the speaker, air in the cup is set in motion by the speaker. This causes the plastic wrap to vibrate and makes the salt dance.

You can also do this demonstration as an experiment. Divide the class into groups of four and supply each group with the materials used in the demonstration. Have the students experiment with different volumes and stations.

A CUPFUL OF MUSIC

Purpose

To show that a paper or plastic cup can amplify sound.

What You Need

For the demonstration:
- paper or plastic cup
- record player
- old record (This may be damaged in the demonstration.)
- sewing needle or straight pin
- soda straw
- stapler or tape

Procedure

Lay the cup on its side, and staple or tape the end of the straw to the top side of the cup. Push the needle or pin through the bottom side of the cup until 2 cm of the needle or pin extends down.

(See Figure 39.) Place a record on the record player and start the machine. Holding the free end of the straw, rest the needle gently on the record. The class should be able to hear the recording.

Explain that the tiny grooves in the record cause the needle to vibrate. Since the needle is attached to the cup, the cup also vibrates. The cup amplifies the sound of the recording. Generally, the larger the cup, the louder the sound.

Figure 39

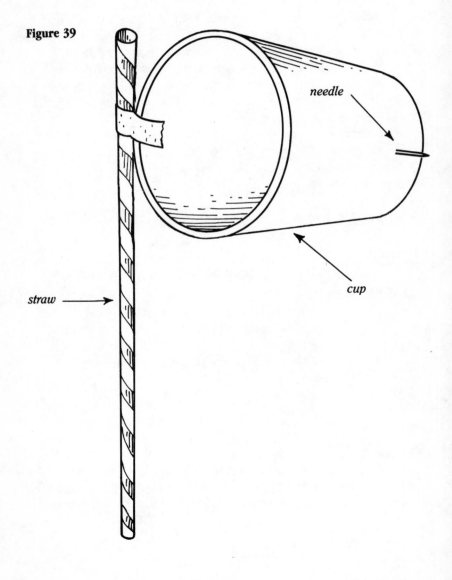

needle

cup

straw

10 | EXPERIENCES WITH WRAPPING AND PACKAGING MATERIALS

Modern technology has provided us with a wide variety of wrapping materials. These include clear plastic wrap, waxed paper, butcher paper, and aluminum foil. Other wrapping materials, such as the clear or colored sheets of acetate film and cellophane, can also be quite useful when teaching science.

There are also numerous materials produced for packing and shipping fragile objects. Some of these are Styrofoam, polyethylene foam, and bubble wrap. Styrofoam can often be found in the form of small pellets and squiggly shapes called popcorn. Polyethylene foams can be found in sheets of various thicknesses. They are quite flexible and are often wrapped around glass containers. Bubble wrap is made of layers of flexible plastic with pockets or bubbles of air trapped between the layers.

BLOCKING OUT SOUND

Purpose

To show that some materials are effective sound insulators. To develop skills in working with variables and recording data.

What You Need

For the class:
- several different types of packing materials (such as bubble wrap, plastic "popcorn," foam "popcorn," polyethylene foam sheets or chips, tissue paper, newspaper, or towels)
- wind-up clock that ticks loudly
- cardboard box (at least 20 × 20 × 20 cm)
- tape recorder with plug-in microphone

Procedure

Start the class by discussing why we might want to be able to block out certain sounds at certain times. For example, when we want to sleep, it would be nice to be able to block out street noises, or when we are in class, it would be nice to block out noise from other rooms and the hallways. Ask students if they can think of any ways to block out sound. Point out that some materials can keep sound from reaching us. These materials are called *noise insulators*. Tell the class that this experiment will help them understand that certain materials help block noise better than others.

Place the ticking clock next to the microphone of the recorder and record the sound for ten seconds. Play back the recorded sound and adjust the volume until the whole class can hear the sound clearly. *Do not* change the volume for the rest of the experiment.

Place the clock in the box and hold the microphone next to the outside of the box. Record the sound for ten seconds. (Make sure that students are quiet during the recording.) Now rewind the tape and play both recordings. Ask students if they hear any difference in the loudness of the sounds. (They will probably find little difference between the two sounds.)

Leave the clock in the box. Surround the clock with one of the packing materials. Record the sound for ten seconds. Then remove the material and test another one. Continue doing this until all the materials have been tested and recorded. (Make sure you hold the microphone the same distance from the box each time you make a recording.) Have students keep a record of the different materials—you might let someone record the name of the material on the tape before you test the material.

After the tests are finished, play the tape back to the class. Ask them to tell you which materials are the most effective sound insulators. (You may have to remind them that the materials that let through the *least* amount of sound are the most effective insulators.)

Explain that sound waves can travel through air, liquids, and most solids. However, some materials tend to absorb the sound waves rather than allow the waves to travel through them. These materials are the best sound insulators and are used to reduce noise in our environment.

A LIQUID RACE

Problem

Will different liquids stick equally to the same surface?

Purpose

To show that different liquids stick to surface materials in different ways. To develop skills in observation, recording data, and controlling variables.

What You Need

For each group of four students:
- 2-3 different wrapping materials (such as aluminum foil, waxed paper, plastic wrap, and butcher paper)
- large book (such as an encyclopedia)
- 4 household liquids in glass or clear plastic containers (preferably liquids with different thicknesses and textures such as oil, milk, catsup, and shampoo)
- 4 droppers
- ruler
- magnifying glass (optional)

Procedure

Encourage the students to examine the liquids. Suggest that they tip the containers slightly to see whether the liquids stick to the sides of the containers. Ask students which liquids seem to stick and which do not. Also ask them if the liquids that stick generally seem thick or thin.

Have students cover the back cover of the book with one of the wrapping materials (foil is a good one to begin with). The covering should be smooth—without wrinkles or folds. Tell students to place one drop of each liquid near the free edge of the covered book cover. The drops should be the same distance from the edge. Have students observe the drops and ask them questions such as, "Are all the drops the same height or do some flatten out?" and "Which drops do you think will stick to the surface and which do you think will run off the surface easily?" You might want students to use magnifying glasses to look at the drops more closely.

Explain to the class that they are going to have a "liquid race." Tell them that they should lift the free edge of the book cover to about a 45° angle so the drops run toward the spine of the book. (See Figure 40.) As soon as one liquid reaches the end of the wrapping material, the students should drop the cover back to its original position. The name of the race winner—the liquid that reaches the edge first—should be recorded. Students should also measure and record the distance that each drop moved from its starting point.

Figure 40

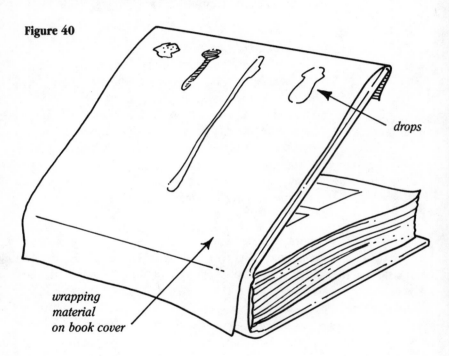

drops

*wrapping
material
on book cover*

When the race is over, have students remove the wrapping material and replace it with a different material. Students should repeat the test, making sure they raise the book cover to about the same height as in the first race. Again, students should measure and record the results of the race. If you wish, another wrapping material may be used for a third race.

Explain to the students that several factors influence the results of the races. First, molecules of matter tend to stick together. For example, molecules of water stick to other molecules of water, which is why a drop of water will "bead" when it is put on a surface such as foil. This attraction between molecules is called *cohesion*. Second, molecules of some materials tend to stick well to molecules of other materials. For instance, catsup sticks well to glass or plastic bottles. This type of attraction is called *adhesion*. The liquid races will usually be won by a liquid that has strong cohesion and little, if any, adhesion to the wrapping material. Such liquids form "firm" drops that roll easily on a surface rather than sticking to it. Liquids that form firm drops that adhere tightly to the surface they are on will move very little when the surface is tilted. And liquids with little cohesion will probably change shape and run in elongated drops or streams on the tilted surface.

If you wish, you can use this activity as an open-ended project. Have students test more than four liquids and different-textured wrapping materials.

CONFUSING COLORS

Problem

Can we identify colors in filtered light?

Purpose

To show that we need white light to see colors accurately.

What You Need

For each pair of students:
- 1 piece each of red, blue, and green acetate or cellophane (Each piece should be 5 × 12 cm.)
- 3 pieces of tagboard (each 20 × 30 cm)
- scissors
- tape
- metric ruler
- white paper

For the class:
- assortment of pastel-colored construction paper (preferably pink, yellow, orange, lavender, light green, and light blue)

Procedure

Have each group of students prepare three "color windows." Tell them to cut a 4 × 10 cm opening in the center of each piece of tagboard. Have students cover the opening on the first piece with red acetate, the second piece with blue acetate, and the third piece with green acetate. (See Figure 41.) Cut the construction paper into paper chips at least 2.5 × 2.5 cm (shape is not important).

Figure 41

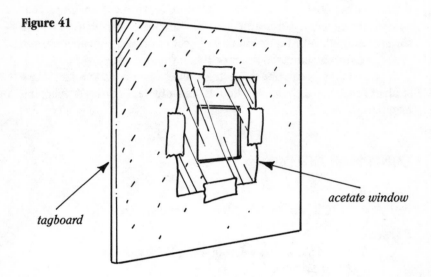

tagboard

acetate window

Lay a piece of white paper on a table and scatter an assortment of paper chips on the paper. Ask a student to pick out all the blue chips. Most students will accomplish this without difficulty. Now ask students if they think they can perform this task while looking through one of the color windows.

Have each group place a white piece of paper on the table at their working station. Tell them to scatter pastel chips on the paper. Direct the students to look through one of the "windows" at the chips and to pick up all the chips of one color. They should place these chips to one side and then look at them in normal light. Ask students if the chips were actually all the same color.

Have students repeat this experiment with the other color windows. Then discuss the results with the class. Students will probably say that the red window made blue and green chips look black or gray, and the pink and yellow chips almost invisible; the blue window made pink and purple chips look almost the same color, and the yellow and orange chips look red-orange; and the green window made the pink and purple chips look gray, and the orange chips look brown.

Explain that we can see color accurately only in white or nearly white light. White light contains all the colors we can see. The color of an object depends on the portion of white light that is reflected. For example, a red shirt looks red because all the colors in the white light that are hitting it are absorbed except for the red light. The red light is reflected into our eyes. When a filter such as a colored piece of acetate or cellophane is placed in front of our eyes, it only allows certain colors of light to pass through it. If you look through red acetate, for example, only red light passes through the filter. Therefore, when you look through a red "window" at a blue chip, the blue pigments are still reflecting blue light back at you, but the red window keeps it from reaching your eyes.

SHRINKING BUBBLES

Problem

What happens to gas when it is cooled below the freezing point of water?

Purpose

To show that a gas contracts when cooled. To develop skills in observation and experimentation.

What You Need

For each student:
— 2 pieces of bubble wrap (at least 10 cm square)
For the demonstration:
— piece of bubble wrap
— bowl filled with water
— pin

Procedure

Show students a sample of the bubble wrap. Ask them what they think is inside the bubbles. If students think there is nothing inside the bubbles, force a piece of the material under the water and prick a bubble with a pin. Have students observe the gas bubbles that rise in the water. Explain that for this experiment it is not necessary to know which gas is in the bubbles.

Hand out the materials to the students. Instruct them to take the pieces of bubble wrap home. They should put one piece in a freezer and the other piece on top of a refrigerator. Tell the students they should wait thirty minutes and then remove the bubble wrap from the freezer and compare it with the other piece. (When first removed from the freezer, the cold sample will appear flatter, since the gas has contracted and the bubbles are less puffed than the warm sample.) Explain that the students must make the comparison quickly, since the small amount of gas in the bubbles heats up fairly quickly.

EXPERIENCES WITH ODDS AND ENDS

There are many materials that can be found in the home and in the classroom that can be used in simple yet instructive science activities. This chapter contains activities that use knitting needles, dollar bills, and Plasticine.

CONDUCTING HEAT

Purpose

To show that heat conducts through some materials and does not conduct through others.

What You Need

For the demonstration:
— 4 metal knitting needles with the same diameter and made of the same material
— candle
— alcohol burner
— 4 pieces corrugated cardboard (each 10 × 15 cm)
— tape
— 2 dimes
— scissors
— tagboard

Procedure

Put a dime under a knitting needle about 10 cm from the pointed end of the needle. Light the candle and let melted wax drip on the coin and needle so the coin sticks to the needle. Make knitting needle supports by cutting a notch in each piece of cardboard and folding the cardboard as shown in Figure 42.

Align two of the needle supports and lay the knitting needle into the notches. The dime should be between the supports, and the pointed end of the needle should extend at least 3 cm from the end of the support.

Figure 42

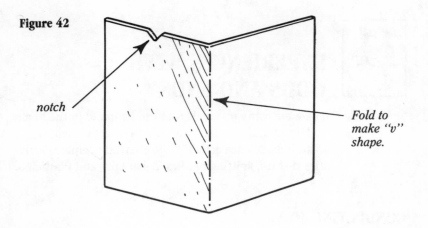

notch

Fold to make "v" shape.

(See Figure 43.) Place the alcohol burner under the pointed end and adjust the flame until it reaches the needle. Ask students to observe the coin. (As the needle is heated, the wax holding the coin will soften and the coin will drop.) Explain that when the needle is heated, the heat moves along (or is conducted along) the needle.

Figure 43

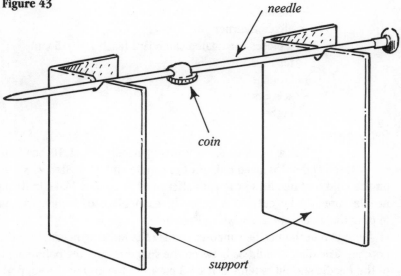

needle

coin

support

Next tape two needles together so the pointed ends overlap about 3 or 4 cm. Tape two more needles together with a piece of tagboard between the needles—the needles should not touch each other. Fasten a dime to each set of needles with dripped wax. The dime should be about 1 cm away from the taped intersections of the needles. Set up the needles on supports as shown in Figure 44. Place the burner under the point where the two sets of needles cross.

Figure 44

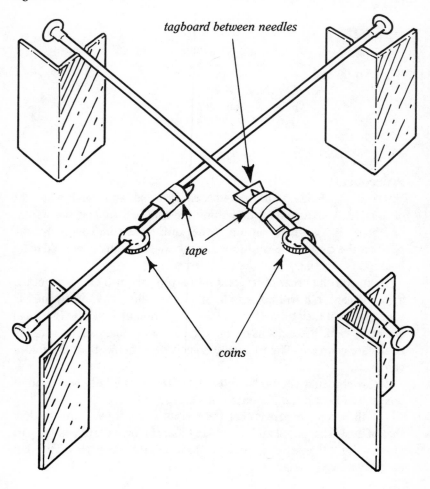

tagboard between needles

tape

coins

Again, have students observe the coins. (The coin on the needles without the tagboard will fall; the other coin will not.) Explain that the tagboard prevents the heat from moving down the needle to the wax. The tagboard worked as a heat insulator—it prevented the heat from moving. Point out that we use this type of insulator every day. For example, pot holders are heat insulators that prevent heat from traveling from a hot pot handle to a person's hand.

HOW STRONG IS A DOLLAR?

Purpose

To demonstrate the supporting strength of a tube.

What You Need

For the demonstration:
- 2 new, crisp one-dollar bills
- 2 index cards (3″ × 5″)
- tape
- several small books

Procedure

Fold one of the index cards in half and stand it upright on a table. Ask students if they think the card will support the weight of a book. Place a book on top of the card. Make sure you center the book on the card. If the card supports the weight of the book, add more books, one at a time, until the card crumples.

Next, roll the other index card into a tube about 2 cm in diameter. Tape the card so it will not unroll. Stand the rolled card on end and ask the students if they think this card will support more or less weight than the other card. Place books on the tube one at a time, making sure the books are centered. The tube will support more books than the folded card.

Show students the dollar bills. Ask them if the bills will support books, too. Repeat the demonstration using the bills.

It will become apparent that the strength of a tube is greater than that of a "v" shaped "shelf." It is likely that the index card will support more weight than the dollar bill. However, the strength of the bill should amaze students.

MAKING IMPRESSIONS

Problem

Can you identify objects from their impressions?

Purpose

To develop skills in observation and drawing conclusions.

What You Need

For the class:
- Plasticine or molding clay

Procedure

This activity is recommended for a science-interest center and should continue as long as there is student interest.

Before class make 10-15 balls of Plasticine about the size of a teaspoon. Flatten each ball to the size of a silver dollar. Press each Plasticine piece onto a small object or surface found in the classroom. For example, you might make impressions of a small section of a radiator grill, of a keyhole, of a hinge, of a paper clip, or of similar objects seen by the students.

Place the impressions and some extra pieces of Plasticine on a table. Challenge students to locate the objects from which the impressions have been made. Tell them they must prove they have found the objects by making their own impressions of them.

An alternative to making Plasticine impressions is to make pencil or crayon rubbings of objects. This works well if you want to include leaves, tree bark, and other objects and surfaces found outdoors. You might want to make eight or ten rubbings and have students try to guess which objects are man-made and which are natural.